INDONESIAN DIP

This sweet and spicy dip is equally at home with grilled chicken satay, a favorite Thai dish.

⅔ cup chunky peanut butter
½ cup firmly packed
  light brown sugar
½ cup fresh lemon juice
¼ cup chili-garlic paste
1 teaspoon soy sauce

•**Combine** all ingredients, and chill 24 hours. Serve with snow peas, Belgian endive, red bell pepper strips, and blanched asparagus. **Yield:** 1½ cups. *Mrs. Paul Smith Longboat Key, Florida*

Street Food

Street Food

Rose Grant

THE CROSSING PRESS
FREEDOM, CALIFORNIA

Editing: Andrea Chesman
Design: Ann Aspell
Illustrations: Elayne Sears

Printed in the United States of America

LIBRARY OF CONGRESS
Library of Congress Cataloging-in-Publication Data

Grant, Rose
    Street food / Rose Grant
        p.   cm.
    Includes index.
    ISBN 0-89594-307-7
    1. Cookery, International.   2. Snack foods.   I. Title
TX725.A1G68 1988
641.59--dc 19
                                                            88-10878
                                                              CIP

*To my sister Marilyn and brother-in-law Abe,
who have always been there for me, and to Betty and Ronnie,
who really understand the meaning of the word "friend."*

Acknowledgments

My special heartfelt thanks go to my editor, Andrea Chesman. Up in the woods of Vermont, far away from busy streets, it was she who first envisioned *Street Food* as a book. I appreciate all of her efforts. Her red pen marks do not show in the final copy, but her intelligence and good taste certainly do.

I would also like to thank my agent, Marlene Connor, for her early enthusiasm and encouragement for the project, when I had my mind on other things.

I am filled with pride and gratitude for my unique family. I would like to thank my husband, Philip, who for more than forty years has been a unique partner and my best friend. He pulled me kicking and screaming into the computer age. His willingness to stop what he was doing to do battle time after time with that humorless machine is yet another example of his abiding faith in the triumph of technology over inept fingers. And I thank my four affable children and lovely daughter-in-law, who became merciless critics. My concepts, my language, my grammar, my spelling, my clichés all met heavy seas under their sharp eyes. I appreciate the time and effort they devoted to shaping me up.

Thanks are also due to my friends on both sides of the Atlantic for listening and adding to my collection of recipes and anecdotes. I am sure that I droned in their ears about street food long after they wanted to talk about something else. If their collective eyes ever glazed over with ennui, I never noticed it.

Contents

Drinks 153

Index 161

Preface

I can resist everything except temptation — Oscar Wilde

There is an old Japanese saying that if you have a happy experience eating something new, your life will be lengthened by seventy-five days. If you take this forecast seriously, the best way to live a long and delicious life is to spend a lot of time sampling street food.

Anyone who has known street food as a child can recall the promise of pleasure that certain foods evoke. Street foods tap into our nostalgia for the past, for simpler times, for holidays and fairs. If you've ever munched on a knish while window shopping in downtown New York, or savored a pan bagnat on the beach in Nice, you've already experienced the pleasure of street food. The first taste of a hot dog at a baseball game, a double-scoop ice cream cone at a fair, roasted chestnuts in a newspaper cone — these are a joyful part of most everyone's childhood memories, something that all people can share.

But *Street Food* is not just for gobble-gulp-and-go. The recipes here make perfect finger food for picnics and patio get-togethers. Dumplings make exotic appetizers. Kebabs served over hot rice become elegant dinner entrées. A spectacular muffuletta or a Philadelphia cheese steak sandwich provides a memorable lunch. And for the eat-after-midnight crowd, a savory onion-filled pissaladière nourishes the body and uplifts the spirit. And what an idea for a unique block party! Ask each guest to prepare one street food, bring it together, and have your own street fair.

Street foods have a rich and colorful history, a bit of which is interwoven among the recipes. From fishwives to royalty, all strata of society have played a role in its evolution. Everyone knows the story of the fourth Earl of Sandwich, who gained immortality because he would not pause to eat while gambling; the sandwich was "invented" to sustain him. But do you know how the pretzel began? Or, how the ice cream cone got started?

It takes a person of great resolve to resist the offerings of street vendors. You are beset by temptations that can make the most jaded palate come alive. It doesn't matter if you are hungry or not. The urge to sample is stimulated by what you see and smell. Your only hope of defying the beckonings of street vendors is knowing that you can make these splendid treats in your own kitchen, where you control the quality and cleanliness of what goes into the dish. You can now enjoy street foods at any time.

My own memories of street foods go back to growing up in New York City. There is nothing, absolutely nothing, that even comes close to the taste of a hot sweet potato on a cold fall evening. One could always tell where the sweet potato man was by looking for the smoke that rose from the creaking handcart he pushed slowly along the street. The smell of the roasting potato started the salivary juices flowing.

The vendor I remember was an old Italian man. The potatoes were kept on a tray, warmed by a wood fire smoldering underneath. Every time he reached into the tray, sparks from the fire rose up the flue. The ritual never varied; the potato was slit on top, salt and butter were added. No verbal exchange in English was possible since he spoke only Italian. But there really was nothing to discuss. Could a slightly scorched sweet potato wrapped in a piece of newspaper really have tasted so good? Sustenance for a penny! The hot potato not only warmed the insides, it warmed the hands as well.

One penny more bought a jelly apple on a stick (also known as a candy apple) from a street vendor pushing a glass-enclosed cart. Here we could choose the one we wanted. Which apple was the biggest? Which seemed to have the thickest layer of red crystallized sugar? Not a decision to be made lightly. Of course our favorite vendor let us change our minds several times before we had to make the final commitment. The first bite told if we had chosen wisely. Was the apple crisp, not mealy? Was the coating crunchy but not impenetrable? We could never agree about the best way to eat a jelly apple and often conducted informal seminars on the subject: to use the teeth to pick off the sugar coating and throw the apple away or to bite into the apple and munch on a mouthful of contrasting tastes and textures.

For a nickel, we could get a charlotte russe, the closest a child could come to the sublime. What exactly was a charlotte russe? It started with a bit of sponge cake in a white fluted cardboard holder. A mound of heavenly whipped cream, sweetened to perfection, covered the sponge cake and spiraled upward in precise swirls. This was topped with half a maraschino cherry. But those were just the ingredients.

Eating a charlotte russe was an acquired skill that took time to perfect. With the first bite one would sink lips, nose, chin into the creamy topping. The approved way to eat this ethereal delicacy was to spoon half the cream into the mouth with a small flat wooden spoon (pros could manage with just the tongue). One then pushed up the rest of the cream and the cake by applying a gentle pressure with the thumbs on the bottom of the cardboard holder and consumed it slowly to make the pleasure last. Rolling the eyes upward at appropriate intervals and murmuring "mmmmmm" seemed to enhance the experience. Of course, the half maraschino cherry was saved for the last bite.

Although the charlotte russe vendors can no longer be found, there is no lack of new entries to take their place. Street foods fit the life-style of a new class of diners called "grazers," those who do not sit down for a meal, but eat here and there while on the move. "Grazing" has become very fashionable. From Wall Street in New York to Ghiradelli Square in San Francisco, vendors offer not only hot dogs and pizza but such exotic temptations as curried goat kebabs and falafel. One can find bagel-o-ramas, where the vendors will put any filling between cut bagel halves, and "melts" of every persuasion vie for attention.

Street vendors are not burdened with a passion for authenticity; they tend to adapt to what is easiest and what keeps well. In this collection, I have tried to include authentic examples of the foods of the various countries but I, too, have had to consider the tastes of people today, and what ingredients are easily available in most large cities. It is fine to suggest that shish kebabs be basted with melted suet from the fat surrounding the tail of the sheep. Though it might have an authentic taste, it is much easier to find this suet in the mountain villages of Greece than in London or Los Angeles. Here, basting with a lemon-oil marinade is an adaptation.

The recipes in *Street Food* have been organized by how the food is eaten (on a stick, in a sandwich, stuffed into a pastry, and so on) rather than along ethnic lines. In many cases the origins of a particular dish are blurred, with several countries claiming to be the true place of birth. Who was *really* first, if it matters at all, is a question best left to historians. All cultures have made a contribution to our food pleasures. As devotees of good food, our mission is easy: just enjoy all of it.

Street Food

Introduction

Nowhere is the melting-pot character of the United States more visible than in its street food. Each wave of immigration brought its own ethnic specialties, many of which were first introduced to mainstream America on the street. People who are fortunate enough to live among diverse cultures may have gotten their first taste of souvlakia or tempura or knishes on the street.

Street foods go back thousands of years to the time when vendors pushed small carts offering nuts and seeds along the dusty byways of ancient Greece. A charcoal fire with a chimney at one end of the cart and a circular pan filled with the freshly roasted nuts and seeds at the other made the rounds of tavernas where people enjoyed a glass of wine.

Bread, local produce, and savory pies appeared on the streets very early. In Europe, the earliest street vendors gathered at crossroads where people traveled. Food sellers would place their wares in large baskets. These baskets were carried on their heads or were suspended from ropes around their necks. The more entrepreneurial merchants diversified. They fashioned for themselves a yoke, which hung on their shoulders; then they could offer several choices from baskets or barrels suspended from the yoke.

In the twelfth and thirteenth centuries, cooking facilities were limited because not many poor people had their own fireplaces. In the cities, fire was so scarce that those who had it were able to sell space to others to have their food heated on it. People soon discovered that it was easier to buy food from a vendor than to stoke up the fire in the fireplace or rent a fire from someone else. Besides, if they bought from a vendor, they had a choice, depending on their mood and pocketbook. Since the poor spent so much time in the street, especially in warmer climates, the evolution of street food was inevitable.

In medieval times, practically all food was eaten with the hands; spoons and forks were still to be introduced. But here and there a few refinements were emerging. Flat pieces of bread called trenchers were used as plates, and the well-mannered now wiped their hands on some bits of cloth instead of on the dog.

Since most everything was finger food, some of the medieval injunctions concerning etiquette might still be appropriate. A German courtesy book of the thirteenth century states: "Let thy hands be clean. Thou must not put thy fingers into thine ears or thy hands on thy head. The man who is eating must not be cleaning by scraping with his fingers any foul part." The foul part in this case meant spots or stains on the clothing. Further instructions about blowing, scraping, and scratching are no longer pertinent—one hopes.

Keeping the hands clean was a minor problem compared to dealing with the refuse that accumulated in the streets. Not many people think of paying homage to the first street cleaners, or even know that in fifteenth-century London, pigs were encouraged to roam the street markets to eat the garbage. (The thought of paying people to clean up did not come until much later.) There was a perfect symbiosis: the pigs were well nourished and the streets were kept clean. Well, sort of. If the pig was a finicky eater, part of the refuse remained. And, if occasionally a pig became entangled with a horse's legs and caused an accident, that just added to the color and excitement of the market.

The market was the center of social life, where activities often lasted from noon to midnight. One could have a tooth pulled, bet on a cockfight, observe a new prize fighter take on the locals, buy mushy peas in a poke, and buy or sell anything, including a wife (circa 1790).

Street markets developed their own folklore and occupational hazards. The expression "to shout like a fish-wife" goes back to the time when the wives of English fishermen sold mussels and whelks on the street at top voice. Street vendors needed a piercing voice to advertise their presence. Often they would bang a large drum or a tambourine to attract attention and drown out competitors. It was also thought that a deafening noise close to the ear stimulated the flow of salivary juices. And banging the drum saved their voices. Just as dancers can dance only as long as their legs hold out, the strength of the vendors' vocal chords determined how long they could sell. When they could no longer holler, they were out of business.

Some claim that the ultimate street markets can be found in Turkey. Since religious Turks drink no alcoholic beverages, they pay extra attention to eating. On the streets of Istanbul, one can see a whole lamb mounted vertically on a spit. The lamb has been rubbed with onion juice, garlic, salt, and pepper. As it slowly roasts, it is basted with the drippings that have been caught in a pan. The vendor cuts off slices, lightly sprinkles them with cinnamon, and places them in a warm pita bread. Fried potatoes and olives make a delicious accompaniment. Like the tune of the Pied Piper, the aroma of the roasting lamb is supposed to be irresistible to anyone downwind.

In Lima, Peru, outside the Plaza de Toros, the second oldest bull ring in the world, there is sure to be a vendor selling kebabs called "anticuchos." This scene has not changed in centuries. The aroma of the beef heart, which has been marinated with at least 15 cloves of crushed garlic, fresh hot peppers, and cumin and is served with deep-fried sweet potatoes and a beer, may be enough to make you forget that beef heart is not one of your favorite foods. Originally llama hearts were used, but llamas are in short supply these days.

The Japanese first gave voice to the idea that we eat with our eyes as well as our mouths. You have only to look at the carts of the street vendors throughout Japan to prove the point. Each vendor is a specialist: yakitori, teriyaki, tempura, noodles. First the eye is teased by the beauty of the presentation, then the palate is drawn in by the seductive scents that waft up on the fragrant steam.

Food wagons offering snacks make their rounds on Japanese streets late at night to tantalize insomniacs. The wagons are portable grills on which fish, potatoes, eggs, and soy bean curd are prepared. The mingled perfumes of the frying foods are carried on the breeze, making sleep impossible until the hunger god has been appeased. A cup of sake provided by the vendor encourages sweeter dreams.

Throughout Thailand, street food is sold by street vendors, some of whom still wear a yoke on their shoulders with two hanging baskets, as they did hundreds of years ago. They have a special gait that they develop to match the springiness of the yoke. Food and condiments are carried in one basket, a barely smoldering charcoal grill in the other. Each vendor is a specialist. You signal the vendor of your choice and have your food cooked on the spot.

Since vendors carry their banked fire with them in a basket, they have to be able to blow it up with just their breath. The fire goes from smoldering embers to high heat almost instantly and cooks the food straightaway. The Thais don't eat three meals a day; they seem to eat one continuous meal all day long, whatever suits their fancy at the moment: soup, satay, noodles of every kind, exotic fruits that refresh the palate.

In Bangkok, there is a flourishing floating market along the canals, which are called *klongs*. The vendors are usually women, and Buddha help the man who gets in their way. Each one sits in a narrow boat close to the banks of the *klong* with her own fire on board. When you signal the vendor of your choice, she is at your side in a second. There seems to be some jockeying for the best position, but it is not clear to the observer how decisions about who sits where are made.

Since these waterside vendors usually sell only one kind of food, the more enterprising ones pull up to the banks in twos or threes to give their customers a chance to mix and match. There seems to be a camaraderie among the vendors that exists in spite of the spirited competition, but then few understand the local dialects. Maybe it is best that foreigners do not understand what one vendor is saying to the other.

On a street market in Bangkok, you might think you see something that looks like roasted spiders. You are correct. If you want to try them, be sure to dip them in salt, as most refined Thais do. Only the peasants eat them plain.

As free markets expand in the cities throughout China, people who work all day at one job become food vendors at night. About 8 o'clock every evening, they set up food stalls that convert an ordinary "people's park" (solid concrete the size of three football fields without a single tree or bench) into a major street extravaganza.

Woks embedded in large drums filled with white hot coals and charcoal braziers appear by the hundreds. A cloud of fragrant smoke works its magic as people converge to meet and eat. Some of the more creative vendors set up a small table and a few chairs to make you think you are in a restaurant. But most people prefer to eat while strolling along.

As you explore the area, looking for the most tempting fare, you have to make quick decisions. If it looks good, get it on the spot, since it is virtually impossible to find "your vendor" again once you've walked away. There are no markers, no streets, no signs, just vendors with their steaming woks as far as the eye can see.

Street markets can educate, often in unexpected ways. In the many free markets in Shanghai, my biologist husband (who, incidentally, has taught anatomy) noticed large barrels of pinkish orbs about the size of tennis balls. People were buying several at a time and carrying them away wrapped in newspaper.

We weren't sure what was being sold, until my husband figured out from the size and shape that they must be bull testicles; the pink color told him that they were pickled. The thought of sacrificing so many bulls to provide a treat for the people in Shanghai food markets seemed a bit excessive, but we were prepared to chalk it up to cultural differences.

One morning we stopped at the market on the way to visit a Chinese friend. Why don't we ask a vendor to write down the Chinese name of the bull testicles? We could show it to our friend who would confirm that my husband had correctly identified the contents of the vat and that biological truths are universal. It had become a matter of professional honor.

If you think that asking the name of something is easy when there is no common language, I invite you to try it.

The first step was to point to the object and hand the vendor a piece of paper. He smiled knowingly, and wrote down a number; we now knew the price. We shook our heads, "No, no." We want the name, not the price. We tried pointing again more vigorously, shouting, smiling. That didn't do it; we could not convey that we wanted the name of objects in the vat. My husband had an idea: if we identify ourselves, maybe the vendor will understand that we want him to identify what's in the tub.

Pointing to himself and to me, he said with great feeling the only words he had learned in Chinese, "*Wo-man Megoran*"—we are Americans. He then pointed quickly to the tub. Great laughter greeted his disclosure; by now we had gathered a sizable crowd who were watching the charade. I would have loved to have understood what people were saying to each other about these idiot *Megorans*, who had just identified their country of origin (as if there was any doubt) while gesticulating at a barrel. I was ready to abandon the whole project when someone in the crowd figured out

what we wanted. A few words were exchanged and some Chinese characters were written on the paper. We nodded "thank you," waved good-by, and left with as much dignity as we could muster.

When we met our friend (also a biologist), the first thing my husband did was to proudly present the paper. He looked like someone who had just been elected to the Society of Culinary Sleuths as he announced with a great flourish, "Pickled bull testicles." Our Chinese friend studied the scrap of paper. "No," he replied, "you are mistaken. These are pickled cabbages." He was much too polite to add that neurobiologists who dabble in anatomy should first learn the difference between bulls and cabbages.

Food on a Stick

The only way ancients could cook their meat was to place the whole animal on a large spit and roast it over an open fire. People who did not have a whole animal to roast made do with bits of meat roasted on a small stick.

Almost every ethnic group has its own version of meat-on-a-stick. It is commonly thought to have started in Greece, but it's a waste of time trying to convince a Turk or an Afghan of this. Moreover, a historian defending the honor of Japanese cuisine could argue that teriyaki predates Middle Eastern kebabs. Kebab is the Turkish name for skewered meat. But the word now transcend all cultures, and you can find kebabs from Italy to Indonesia.

The distinctive flavor of each country is imparted by a particular blend of marinating ingredients. Though each recipe varies, there are some basic combinations. Soy sauce, sake, and sugar are almost always used for yakitori. Soy sauce, garlic, molasses, and peanuts mean that a dish is an Indonesian satay. Lemon and oregano tell you it's a Greek souvlakia.

Charcoal was used for cooking very early on, especially in warmer climates, where large open fire cooking would have been intolerable. Barbecuing (the word comes from Mexico where the roasting frame used for large joints of meat was called *barbacoa*) has become almost a generic term for charcoal broiling. The only piece of equipment required is a grill. A simple hibachi works as well as the most elaborate patio equipment. A long-handled basting brush prevents scorched fingers. Broiling the kebabs in the oven is almost as good, but the charcoal fire imparts a special flavor that cannot be duplicated.

If you are serious about kebab cooking, it would be useful to have a supply of 6-inch and 12-inch wooden or bamboo skewers. The skewers should be soaked in water for 30 minutes before use to prevent them from catching fire. Metal skewers work as well, but the wooden ones are more authentic for street food. A vendor's trick is to place the meat on the skewer before marinating it. This works well for large quantities because it cuts down handling time when you are trying to get many skewers on the fire at the same time. All the kebabs in this book are made on 12-inch skewers.

A marinating trick that can be used with any recipe is to do the marinating in a self-sealing plastic bag. It is easy to turn the bag over and over, which covers all the pieces evenly with the marinade.

Souvlakia

The Greek word for spit is souvla, *so anything grilled on a spit (chunks of lamb or pork, ground meats, chicken, even seafood) is called* souvlakia. *The meat sits in the marinade absorbing the flavors until it is grilled on a charcoal fire.*

⅓ cup olive oil
¼ cup lemon juice
¼ cup dry red wine
3 garlic cloves, minced
3 large bay leaves, cut in half
2 pounds lean lamb (from the leg), cut into 1-inch cubes
Salt and pepper
2 teaspoons dried imported oregano (or Greek wild marjoram)
3 onions, quartered

In a bowl, combine the olive oil, lemon juice, wine, garlic, and bay leaves for the marinade. Sprinkle the lamb with salt, pepper, and oregano. Put the lamb in the marinade and place in the refrigerator for 12 to 24 hours. Turn the lamb every few hours to be sure the marinade covers all the meat.

Remove the meat from the marinade and place on 6 prepared wooden skewers, along with the onion quarters and the bay leaf halves. Grill the meat over white hot coals for 10 minutes on each side, basting with the marinade. Do not let the meat get overdone. It should be pink on the inside. Discard the bay leaves before serving.

Serve with a Greek salad topped with feta cheese and black olives and warm pita bread. A robust red wine or retsina, the Greek wine, makes it a memorable meal.

Souvlakia Keftaides

To transform these meatball kebabs into delicious cocktail party fare, broil the meatballs without the skewer and serve hot, speared on a toothpick.

1½ tablespoons minced fresh parsley
½ cup finely minced onion
2 tablespoons fresh minced oregano or 1 teaspoon dried
2 tablespoons fresh minced mint or 1 teaspoon dried
2 eggs, beaten
1½ teaspoons salt
¾ teaspoon black pepper
½ cup pine nuts (pignoli)
2 pounds ground lean beef or lamb
Juice of 1 lemon

Combine the parsley, onion, oregano, mint, eggs, salt, pepper, and pine nuts with the ground meat. Using your fingers, shape the mixture into 18 thin sausages, each about 2 inches long. Thread 3 sausages along their lengths on each of 6 prepared wooden skewers and grill them over white hot coals. The meat should be cooked very quickly, no more than 5 minutes on each side. The keftaides should be brown on the outside but still pink inside. Sprinkle with the lemon juice. If you like, serve with pita bread.

Shrimp Kebabs with Feta

Shrimp (or other seafood) kebabs replace meat on Greek islands, where the fresh catch is brought in daily.

½ cup olive oil
½ cup fresh lemon juice
3 garlic cloves, minced
2 tablespoons chopped fresh thyme or 1 teaspoon dried
2 tablespoons chopped fresh oregano or 1 teaspoon dried
1 tablespoon grated lemon peel
½ teaspoon sugar
Salt and freshly ground pepper
20 large shrimp (about 1¼ pounds)
8 cherry tomatoes
8 large mushrooms, stems removed
½ cup crumbled feta cheese (optional)

In a bowl, combine the oil, lemon juice, garlic, thyme, oregano, lemon peel, sugar, and salt and pepper to taste. Add the shrimp and marinate, covered, in the refrigerator for several hours.

Thread the shrimp onto 4 prepared wooden skewers, pushing them to the end of the skewer. Reserve the marinade. Place the skewers on a charcoal grill over white hot coals and cook for 3 to 5 minutes on each side, basting frequently with the marinade. Or, broil the kebabs in the oven on a baking sheet, 4 inches from the heat. As with all seafood, do not overcook. When the shrimp are almost done, thread the tomatoes and mushroom caps onto the opposite ends of the skewers. Return to the heat for another 2 minutes. Serve hot in a warmed pita pocket topped with crumbled feta cheese.

Food on a Stick

Caucasian Shashlik

The word shashlik *is like the word "steak" in that it gives very little information. Russian shashlik varies from one region to another. Caucasian shashlik has a different flavor from the Georgian version, which is traditionally served with pomegranate syrup. These kebabs are only distantly related to the shashlik of Uzbekistan, which is perfumed with fresh cilantro and dill.*

2 pounds lean lamb (from the leg), cut into 1-inch cubes (reserve very thin slices of fat trimmed from the meat)
1 large onion, chopped
3 garlic cloves, minced
½ cup red wine vinegar
¼ cup water
½ teaspoon ground cloves
½ teaspoon cinnamon
10 black peppercorns, crushed
½ cup red wine
3 tablespoons olive oil
Salt

Combine the lamb cubes, onion, and garlic in a bowl.

In a saucepan, combine the vinegar, water, cloves, cinnamon, and peppercorns. Bring the mixture to a boil and then let it cool. Add the red wine. Pour this marinade over the meat mixture, cover, and let it sit at room temperature for at least 4 hours, turning the meat often. Marinating it in the refrigerator overnight is even better.

Remove the meat and dry each piece of meat with a paper towel. Thread the meat onto 6 prepared wooden skewers, placing several slices of lamb fat between the pieces of meat; this adds additional flavor. Place the skewers on a charcoal grill over white hot coals for 10 to 12 minutes, turning frequently, and brushing with additional oil. The meat should be pink on the inside. Discard the lamb fat and salt to taste just before serving.

Serve with fluffy rice and a salad for a satisfying main dish.

Chinese Pork Kebabs

2 tablespoons peanut oil
2 teaspoons finely minced
  fresh ginger root
4 garlic cloves, minced
3 tablespoons soy sauce
3 tablespoons dry sherry
1 tablespoon miso
1½ tablespoons sugar
1 piece star anise or ½
  teaspoon anise powder
2 pounds boneless pork loin
  or tenderloin, cut into 1-
  inch cubes

In a small skillet over high heat, heat the oil. Add the ginger root and garlic and stir-fry for about 30 seconds. Add the soy sauce, sherry, miso, sugar, and anise and simmer gently over low heat for a few minutes. Cool slightly.

Pour the sauce over the pork cubes and mix well. Let stand for 2 to 3 hours at room temperature or marinate in the refrigerator overnight. Remove the pork from the marinade and thread onto 6 prepared wooden skewers. Place the skewers on a charcoal grill over white hot coals and cook for 7 to 10 minutes on each side, turning and basting occasionally.

This kebab plus fluffy white rice and a stir-fried vegetable makes a superb meal.

Japanese Tuna Teriyaki

Yield: 6 kebabs

In Japan, when the tuna boats come in, the street vendors appear. Only the very freshest tuna is used for teriyaki; otherwise, it is not worth doing.

2 pounds tuna, cut into 24 one-inch cubes
¾ cup Japanese soy sauce
2 tablespoons sugar
2 garlic cloves, minced
2 large scallions, minced
1 teaspoon minced fresh ginger root

Place the tuna in a bowl. Combine the soy sauce, sugar, garlic, scallions, and ginger root and mix well. Pour over the tuna and stir to coat. Marinate in the refrigerator for 1 hour (or less). Drain the fish, reserving the marinade.

Thread the tuna onto 6 prepared wooden skewers. Place the skewers on a charcoal grill over white hot coals. Grill for about 5 minutes; turn and grill for another 5 minutes, basting occasionally with the marinade. The kebabs can also be broiled in the oven on a baking sheet 4 inches from the heat.

Chicken Yakitori

Yield: 6 kebabs

Teriyaki and yakitori are first cousins. Both are skewered meat, grilled over a charcoal fire; both use similar sauces. The only difference is that teriyaki is marinated while yakitori is just basted with sauce as it is grilled.

¾ cup soy sauce
¾ cup sake (Japanese wine)
¼ cup sugar
2 pounds chicken breasts, skinless and boneless, cut into twenty-four 1½-inch cubes
6 large, thin scallions, white part only, cut into 2-inch lengths
Cayenne pepper

Mix the soy sauce, sake, and sugar in a bowl. Dip the chicken and scallions into the mixture. Drain, reserving the sauce. Thread the chicken onto 6 prepared wooden skewers. Grill the kebabs over white hot coals for 8 to 10 minutes, turning often and basting frequently with the soy sauce mixture. Sprinkle with cayenne pepper to taste just before serving.

Tikka Kobobs

Tikka *means spicy. All Indians cooks have an opinion about how spicy a particular dish should be. A good part of meal preparation is devoted to combining the spices to get just the correct blend. Commercial blends, known as curry powder, are available, but not many self-respecting Indian cooks would use it, except in an emergency. I was told, "It's like using a cake mix."*

2 pounds lean lamb, cut into
    1-inch cubes
1½ cups thick unflavored
    yogurt
2 teaspoons garam masala
1 teaspoon ground coriander
½ teaspoon ground turmeric
2 garlic cloves, crushed
½ teaspoon ground nutmeg
¼ teaspoon ground cloves
1 teaspoon (more or less)
    chili powder
2 teaspoons ground cumin
Grated peel and juice of 2
    lemons

Place the lamb cubes in a large bowl. Mix the yogurt with all the other ingredients. Add to the lamb. Cover and marinate at least overnight in refrigerator, or up to 2 days. Remove the meat from the marinade and thread onto 6 prepared wooden skewers. Grill over white hot coals for 8 to 10 minutes, turning frequently. Do not over-cook; the meat should still be pink inside.

Garnish with onion rings and lemon wedges. These kobobs are usually served with Indian breads—nan or chappati—or a pita.

Satay Ajam

There are many versions of this Indonesian skewered chicken. It is served with Katjang Saos (Indonesian peanut butter sauce) for dipping. The hotness of the sauce can be varied by increasing or decreasing the amount of chili powder and Tabasco sauce.

Served with noodles and a cucumber salad, Satay Ajam makes a satisfying main dish.

2 garlic cloves, minced
3 tablespoons fresh lime juice
½ teaspoon salt
½ teaspoon black pepper
2 teaspoons brown sugar
½ cup soy sauce
1 tablespoon molasses
2 tablespoons minced fresh cilantro (fresh coriander or Chinese parsley)
2 pounds chicken breasts, skinned and boned, cut into 1½-inch cubes
3 tablespoons vegetable oil

In a bowl, combine the garlic, lime juice, salt, pepper, sugar, soy sauce, molasses, and cilantro. Add the chicken cubes and marinate for several hours at room temperature, or overnight in the refrigerator.

Thread the chicken onto 6 prepared wooden skewers and grill over white hot charcoal for 5 minutes on each side. Brush with the oil several times while grilling.

Katjang Saos

1 cup peanut butter
¼ cup chopped scallions
2 garlic cloves, minced
1 tablespoon fresh lemon juice
¼ cup soy sauce
1 tablespoon minced fresh ginger root
¼ teaspoon chili powder
Dash Tabasco sauce

In a blender or food processor, combine the peanut butter, scallions, and garlic. Process until smooth. Add the lemon juice, soy sauce, ginger, chili powder, and Tabasco. Heat in a saucepan until hot. If it is too thick, a little water can be added. Serve hot. Makes 2 cups.

Marinated Pork Satays

Yield: 6 satays

This, too, is an Indonesian recipe. Flavorful pork makes a delicious satay. The pork can be flattened for a more authentic look or left in 1-inch cubes.

¼ cup soy sauce
1 onion, finely minced
2 garlic cloves, minced
2 tablespoons lime juice
1 fresh chili pepper, seeded and chopped
1 tablespoon finely minced fresh ginger root
2 pounds lean pork, cut into 1-inch cubes

Combine the soy sauce, onion, garlic, lime juice, chili pepper, and ginger root. Add the pork and toss to coat. Marinate for 2 to 12 hours, covered, in the refrigerator. Longer marinating intensifies the flavor.

Remove the pork from the marinade and reserve the marinade. Thread the meat onto 6 prepared skewers. Grill over white hot coals for 12 to 15 minutes on each side, basting with the marinade and turning frequently. Katjang Saos, the peanut sauce served with Satay Ajam (page 16), combines beautifully with these pork satays.

Bangkok Pork Satays

Yield: 6 satays

This is a Thai version of pork on a stick. Peanuts and pork make an unbeatable combination. The dipping sauce is served separately.

2 pounds boneless pork, cut
   into 1-inch cubes
¼ cup smooth peanut butter
1 teaspoon ground coriander
1 teaspoon salt
1 teaspoon ground cumin
½ teaspoon black pepper
3 medium-size onions, finely
   chopped
2 garlic cloves, minced
3 tablespoons lemon juice
1 tablespoon brown sugar
3 tablespoons soy sauce

1 garlic clove, chopped
1 small onion, chopped
1 cup peanuts, coarsely
   chopped
2 dried hot chili peppers
2 pieces candied ginger
½ teaspoon salt
½ teaspoon turmeric
Juice of ½ lemon
1 cup water
Coconut milk

Place the pork cubes in a bowl. Mix together the peanut butter, coriander, salt, cumin, pepper, onions, garlic, lemon juice, sugar, and soy sauce and add to the pork. Marinate in the refrigerator for several hours or overnight. Drain and reserve the marinade.

Thread the pork onto 6 prepared wooden skewers and grill over white hot coals for 15 to 20 minutes, turning frequently and basting with the marinade.

Dipping Sauce

Combine all the sauce ingredients, except the coconut milk, in a food processor or blender. Process until smooth. Place the mixture in the top of a double boiler and cook over simmering water for 30 minutes. If the sauce is too thick, thin with coconut milk, which can be bought or made by combining 2 cups hot milk with 1 cup freshly grated coconut. When the mixture has cooled, drain off the coconut milk and discard the solids. Press the grated coconut with the back of a spoon to be sure to extract all the coconut milk.

Let the sauce stand for 30 minutes, then strain and reheat. Serve the sauce in a separate bowl along with the satays and hot rice.

Philippine Barbecued Pork

Yield: 4 kebabs

1 pound fresh pork butt,
  sliced ½-inch thick
½ cup Chinese barbecue
  sauce or hoisin sauce
3 tablespoons red wine
  vinegar
3 garlic cloves, crushed
Juice of 1 lime
Salt and pepper

Cut the meat into ¾-inch cubes. Combine the barbecue sauce, vinegar, garlic, lime juice, and salt and pepper to taste. Thread the meat onto 4 prepared skewers. Place the meat and the marinade in a glass or ceramic pan. Place in the refrigerator and marinate overnight, turning a few times. Remove the kebabs from the marinade and place over white hot coals. Grill for 10 minutes on each side, basting frequently.

South Pacific Chicken

Yield: 6 kebabs

If you are ever traveling in the Fiji Islands and find yourself on the streets of Tonga, be sure to try their version of the ubiquitous chicken kebab. Along with your kebab you will be served the dipping sauce in a small saucer. You stand around the stall, dipping and eating. After you finish your kebab, you return the saucer to the vendor for the next customer.

This recipe is a modern adaptation; instant chicken bouillon granules add flavor and texture.

½ cup finely chopped
  peanuts
3 tablespoons chicken stock
  granules
4 scallions, with some of the
  green, chopped
½ teaspoon salt
½ cup lime juice
2 cups sour cream or yogurt
  (or half of each)
2 pounds chicken breasts,
  cut into 1½-inch cubes

Mix together the nuts, chicken stock granules, scallions, and salt. Add just enough of the lime juice to make thick paste. Combine half of this nut paste with the sour cream and remaining lime juice. Set aside; this is the dipping sauce.

Thread the chicken cubes onto 6 prepared wooden skewers. Roll each skewer in the remaining nut paste, coating the chicken with the nut mixture. Refrigerate for 2 to 3 hours, or longer. Grill over white hot coals for 8 to 10 minutes, turning often. Serve with the sauce for dipping.

Caribbean Kebabs

In the Caribbean, pineapple juice is used as a tenderizing agent. As it penetrates the meat, the juice adds its own delicious flavor.

On the streets of Anguilla, these kebabs would be much smaller, with very small pieces of meat and vegetables on the same skewer.

½ cup unsweetened
   pineapple juice
¼ cup white vinegar
2 tablespoons molasses
1 small onion, chopped
2 garlic cloves, finely
   chopped
1 tablespoon Dijon-style
   mustard
Salt and pepper
2 pounds top sirloin, cut into
   1½-inch cubes
15 small white onions
15 cherry tomatoes
3 medium-size green
   peppers, cut into 1½-inch
   squares
15 one-inch cubes fresh
   pineapple

In a bowl, combine the pineapple juice with the vinegar, molasses, onion, garlic, mustard, and salt and pepper to taste. Add the beef cubes and marinate at room temperature for several hours, or in the refrigerator overnight. Drain and reserve the marinade to be used a basting sauce.

Drop the onions into boiling water for 1 to 2 minutes. Slip off the skins.

Thread the meat onto 3 prepared wooden skewers, pushing the pieces close together. Thread the onions, tomatoes, green peppers pieces, and pineapple cubes alternately on 3 other skewers. Brush all the skewers with the marinade. Grill the meat over white hot coals for 12 to 15 minutes, turning twice. Brush with additional marinade at each turning. Grill the vegetable-fruit skewers for about 5 minutes, basting with marinade once. Watch them; they burn easily.

Jamaican Curried Goat

Curried goat is the national dish of Jamaicans. It is sold by vendors all over that island and wherever homesick Jamaicans gather. Goat meat is distinctive in that it is sweet and slightly gamy at the same time. Leg of lamb can be substituted if your butcher is out of young goat.

2 pounds goat leg or loin, cut into 1-inch cubes
⅓ cup peanut oil
2 garlic cloves, minced
2 medium-size tomatoes, peeled, seeded, and coarsely chopped
2 medium-size onions, chopped
2 scallions, with some of the green, chopped
2 small hot green Anaheim chilies, minced
2 (or more) tablespoons curry powder
1 teaspoon salt
½ teaspoon ground pepper

Place the meat in a large bowl. Combine the oil, garlic, tomatoes, onions, scallions, chilies, curry powder, salt, and pepper. Pour over the meat and mix well. Marinate in the refrigerator for several hours.

Remove the meat from the marinade and reserve the marinade. Thread the meat onto 8 prepared skewers. Grill over white hot coals for 25 to 30 minutes, or until tender, turning frequently and basting with the marinade.

Mixed Grill Kebabs

These kebabs can be found on the street in towns in northern Italy. A similar version can be found on the French Riviera. The combination of tastes and textures make this a particularly delicious kebab.

6 small spicy pork sausage
  links
6 slices lean bacon
½ pound chicken livers, cut
  in half
6 small white onions
¼ cup fresh lemon juice
⅓ cup olive oil
1½ teaspoons mixed dried
  Italian herbs
Salt and pepper
2 large garlic cloves, minced
2 tablespoons Worcestershire
  sauce
2 tablespoons soy sauce
2 tablespoons Dijon-style
  mustard
1 whole boneless and skinless
  chicken breast, cut into 6
  pieces
6 small fresh mushroom caps

Place the sausages in a skillet and fry them for about 5 minutes, until half done. Remove them from the skillet and drain on paper towels. Place the bacon in the same skillet and fry for a few minutes, until half done. Do not let it get crisp. Remove from the pan and drain on paper towels. Wrap the bacon around the chicken livers.

Drop the onions into boiling salted water and cook for 1 to 2 minutes, until just tender. Do not overcook. Drain and peel.

Mix together the lemon juice, oil, Italian herbs, salt and pepper to taste, garlic, Worcestershire, soy sauce, and mustard. This is the basting sauce.

Thread 6 prepared skewers with the chicken, sausage, chicken livers wrapped in bacon, mushrooms, and onions. Place on a charcoal grill over white hot coals. Grill for 6 to 8 minutes on each side, basting frequently with the basting sauce. Or broil the kebabs in the oven on a baking sheet, 4 inches from the heat, basting often.

Sausages: It Started with the Ancients

It is not clear who first thought of stuffing ground meat into a casing, but sausages go back a long way. Babylonians had their version of the sausage 3500 years ago. Homer sang of sausage in *The Odyssey*. The Romans had a delicacy made of ground pork and pine nuts that became a part of their pagan orgies. When Constantine the Great came to power, he decided that sausages were too good for plebian consumption and banned them for the lower classes.

The word sausage comes from the Latin *salsus*; it means salty. As sausages became more popular, they changed in character; they were no longer considered a delicacy. In Victorian times they were known as "little bags of mystery" for obvious reasons. Meats of questionable origin and unpopular organ meats found their way into the sausage mixture. Strong herbs and spices, especially pepper, were added to conceal what needed hiding. The meat was then stuffed into the cleaned intestine of a pig, sheep, or goat. Smoking the sausages preserved them and disguised questionable flavors.

Every country has its own sausage. Haggis has nourished the Scots for hundreds of years. This sausage is almost all organ meat and oatmeal stuffed into a sheep's stomach, so skillfully flavored that you would never guess that it is good for you. In some countries, sausages have become delicacies once again. They are made of the finest meat, enhanced by black and green peppercorns, pistachios, truffles, garlic, and a wide variety of spices.

Many cities are renown for their sausages, including Frankfurt, Bologna, and Genoa, to name just a few. Everyone has heard of the salami but not everyone knows, except on the Greek island of Salamis, that the world-famous salami originated there.

A grilled merguez, the small spicy Algerian sausage that has made its way from Morocco to the streets of Paris, garlicky Portuguese linguica, or a German bratwurst on a skewer are the easiest of street foods; there is nothing to do except grill them over a charcoal fire. And lest I offend the southern half of the United States, it should be pointed out that corn dogs are not to be missed.

Grilled Pork and Sausage

Yield: 8 kebabs

You would be likely to find this kebab in Portuguese neighborhoods. The spiciness depends on the linguica, which can be mild or loaded with garlic and spices.

This combination produces a superb kebab. The kebabs can be broiled in the oven instead of grilled; they will be almost as good.

1 tablespoon finely chopped garlic
2 teaspoons Hungarian paprika
1 teaspoon cinnamon
1 teaspoon salt
½ teaspoon freshly ground black pepper
1 large bay leaf, crumbled
1 teaspoon grated orange peel
1 orange, unpeeled, thinly sliced
½ cup dry white wine
¼ cup water
1½ pounds lean boneless pork, cut into 1½-inch cubes
1 pound Portuguese linguica (any garlicky smoked pork sausage can be substituted)

In a bowl, mix together the garlic, paprika, cinnamon, salt, pepper, bay leaf, orange peel, orange slices, wine, and water. Add the cubes of pork. Coat them with the marinade. Cover. Marinate the pork at room temperature for 4 to 8 hours, or in the refrigerator for 24 hours, tossing every few hours.

Cut the linguica crosswise into ½-inch rounds. Remove the pork from the marinade and thread onto 8 prepared skewers, pushing the pieces close together. Leave room on each skewer for the linguica to be added. Place on a charcoal grill over white hot coals. Grill for about 10 minutes, turning frequently and brushing with the marinade. Add the linguica pieces to each skewer and continue grilling, basting, and turning for another 10 minutes.

Serve with Portuguese bread.

Crusty Corn Dogs

Yield: 8 corn dogs

This southern U.S. favorite has traveled well. You can find corn dogs on the streets of New York and San Francisco. Children have adopted corn dogs and scarf them down with great pleasure whenever they can.

Oil for deep frying
8 all-beef frankfurters
Flour
¼ cup yellow cornmeal
½ cup sifted flour
¼ teaspoon salt
¼ teaspoon baking soda
½ cup buttermilk
1 egg
Spicy mustard or catsup

Preheat 2 inches of oil in a deep-fat fryer or heavy-bottom saucepan to 375° F. Meanwhile, insert a prepared wooden skewer into the end of each frankfurter and roll the frankfurter in the flour to coat.

Mix together the cornmeal, sifted flour, salt, and baking soda. Beat together the buttermilk and egg and stir into the cornmeal mixture.

Dip the frankfurters in the cornmeal batter to coat. Shake off any excess. Deep fry until golden brown, 2 to 3 minutes. Drain on paper towels. Serve hot and dip in spicy mustard or catsup as you eat.

Sandwiches

Who has not awakened in the middle of the night hankering for some novel concoction between two pieces of bread? Remember the gyros on the streets of Iráklion? Or the falafel sold by the falafel king of Tel Aviv? There in your bed, you can almost inhale the pleasure of a Caribbean stuffed roti. Where are those street vendors just when you need them most? A smoked sausage sandwich, a trencherman-sized hero, a sizzling *croque monsieur* do more than stop the hunger. They appease our nocturnal craving for the exotic, and let us go back to sleep stuffed and satisfied.

Everyone thinks they know how sandwiches began. It was the Earl of Sandwich, a compulsive gambler, who first started eating them so he could appease his hunger pangs without leaving the gaming tables. Well, not exactly. The world's first recorded sandwich was eaten in the first century, when Rabbi Hillel made it part of the Passover dinner. Two pieces of unleavened bread (matzo) were filled with bitter herbs, chopped nuts, and apples and eaten to symbolize the suffering and deliverance of the Jews. This "sandwich" is a part of the Passover seder to this day.

The first open-faced sandwich goes back to the Middle Ages, before plates were invented. Meat and gravy, as well as other foods, were served on thick bread slabs, called trenchers. After the food was eaten, the trencher was often offered to someone less fortunate who was lurking about. The dainty finger sandwiches that grace an elegant buffet go back to this humble beginning.

The sandwich is at home throughout the world and can be eaten at any meal of the day or night. Bagels and cream cheese for breakfast or brunch, a workman's sandwich for lunch, a muffuletta for dinner, sandwiches for picnics, a sandwich of leftovers for a midnight snack.

In the words of Woody Allen, we owe much to the sandwich. It freed mankind from the hot lunch.

Muffulettas

This leaky delicacy was created in the early 20th century. It is a variation of the Italian antipasto, and to this day it is a favorite sandwich in New Orleans. On a balmy day, one can find the lunch-time crowd sitting along the levee, muffuletta in hand; it's a wonder that anybody goes back to work in the afternoon.

It is the combination of olives, pickled vegetables, and spices that give this sandwich its unique flavor and eye appeal. The muffuletta is perfect for picnics; in New Orleans, it is often eaten at football games.

½ cup chopped stuffed green olives

½ cup pitted and chopped dry oil-cured black olives

½ cup mixed pickled vegetables (giardiniera), drained and coarsely chopped

½ cup chopped celery

¼ cup olive oil

¼ cup lemon juice

2 tablespoons minced fresh parsley

2 tablespoons fresh oregano or 1 teaspoon dried

½ teaspoon freshly ground pepper

10-inch round Italian bread, split horizontally

2 garlic cloves, finely minced

¼ pound Italian salami, very thinly sliced

¼ pound provolone cheese, thinly sliced

4 slices prosciutto, very thinly sliced

In a bowl, combine the olives, pickled vegetables, celery, oil, lemon juice, parsley, oregano, and pepper. Cover and refrigerate for 8 hours or overnight, tossing the mixture a few times.

Remove some of the center of the bread. Dampen the inside of the bread with a little juice of the marinade and sprinkle with the minced garlic. On the bottom half of bread, layer the salami, half of the olive mix, the provolone, the remaining half of the olive mix, and top with the prosciutto. Additional garlic can be sprinkled on each layer. Cover with the top half of the bread. Cut into 4 wedges and serve with a cold beer or a glass of wine.

Note: A recent variation is to wrap the wedges in aluminum foil and heat them in a 300° F. oven until the cheese melts, about 5 minutes. Letting the cheese melt and the flavors blend enhances the taste. Serve at once.

New Orleans Hamburgers

Yield: 4 hamburgers

The combination of hot seasonings and chopped fried onions make this hamburger something special. In New Orleans, if you order it "dressed," it will be done up with shredded lettuce, tomato and pickle slices, and a lot of mayonnaise.

1 tablespoon vegetable oil
1½ cups chopped onions
1 long French bread loaf
1 pound very lean ground
  beef
1½ teaspoons salt
½ teaspoon freshly ground
  pepper
⅛ teaspoon cayenne pepper
½ teaspoon paprika
¼ teaspoon chili powder
  (more if desired)

In a medium-sized skillet, heat the oil. Add the onions and fry until the onions are glazed.

In a large bowl, combine the ground beef, the fried onions, and seasonings. Mix well with a wooden spoon. Shape the meat into 4 patties about ½ inch thick and shaped so they will fit into the French bread.

Place the bread in a 250° F. oven to warm for 10 minutes.

Grill the hamburgers on a hot griddle until brown on both sides, flattening them as they cook. They should be crisp at the edges.

Divide the bread into 4, then slice each piece horizontally. Place the hamburgers on the French bread and pass the "dressings."

Note: The fried onions can be passed separately, instead of incorporating them into the burgers.

Po' Boys

There must be at least ten versions of the "original" po' boy sandwich. Po' boys go back to the time when poor boys in New Orleans would take a roll and put anything they could find into it and eat it on the spot. Potato po' boys and catfish po' boys were most common. Often, French bread was split in half lengthwise and then cut into thirds. Each third was then filled with whatever was around. Fried oysters if they could afford it, tomato and bacon, French sausages, fried eggs, and chicken salad found their way into the po' boy. Crystal Hot Sauce (available in most supermarkets), a New Orleans specialty, was the ubiquitous addition to most sandwiches.

As po' boys got richer, roast beef replaced the fried egg. In this recipe, the roast beef is actually pot roast; the rich gravy is more critical than the meat. The French bread should be warm, right out of the oven, if possible.

1 long loaf fresh French bread
Mayonnaise
1 cup shredded iceberg lettuce
1 pound pot-roasted beef, thinly sliced
1 cup thickened roast beef gravy
2 medium-size tomatoes, thinly sliced
Salt and black pepper
Crystal Hot Sauce (optional)

Warm the bread in a 250° F. oven for 10 minutes, then cut it lengthwise. Spread the bottom half of the bread with mayonnaise. Sprinkle with shredded lettuce. Place slices of beef, slightly overlapping, on top. Cover with thickened gravy. (To thicken gravy, combine 1 tablespoon flour with 2 tablespoons cold water. Add the mixture to 1 cup meat gravy, which has been skimmed of fat, and cook over moderate heat until thick.) Top with slices of tomato and season with salt and pepper and a sprinkling of hot sauce, if desired. Cover with the top of the bread. Serve immediately, with lots of napkins.

Oyster Loaf Po' Boys

Many think this is the ultimate po' boy. According to local opinion it must be made with the local oysters for authenticity.

2 dozen large oysters, shucked and thoroughly drained
2 eggs
½ cup milk
1 teaspoon salt
½ teaspoon black pepper
2 cups stone-ground cornmeal
2 twelve-inch loaves French or Italian bread
6 tablespoons melted butter
Vegetable oil for deep frying
Tartar sauce

Pat the oysters dry. In a small bowl, whisk together the eggs and milk until well blended. In another small bowl, combine the salt and pepper with the cornmeal. Dip the oysters, one at a time, into the egg mixture and then into the cornmeal. Be sure to coat completely. Arrange the oysters on a plate and chill for 1 hour or more.

Cut each bread loaf in half, slice it horizontally, and remove some of the dough center. Brush the bread with melted butter and place on a cookie sheet. Warm the bread in a 250° F. oven for 5 minutes.

Heat the oil to 375° F. Fry the oysters, 6 at a time, for 3 to 4 minutes, turning once. Drain on paper towels.

Place 6 oysters on the bottom half of the bread. Spread with tartar sauce and top with the other half of the bread. Serve the sandwich warm with a cold beer.

Middle Eastern Kofta

This sandwich could have originated in Turkey or Greece or anywhere in that region, except that in Greece it would be called keftethes *instead of* kofta. *Though lamb is the meat most frequently used, beef, or beef mixed with lamb, makes a delicious patty. Seasonings vary from a hint of cinnamon or allspice to cumin, coriander, and mint.*

2 pounds lean ground lamb
  or beef
2 medium-sized onions,
  finely chopped
½ cup bread crumbs
2 teaspoons ground coriander
2 teaspoons ground cumin
2 tablespoons chopped fresh
  oregano or 1 teaspoon
  dried
2 tablespoons chopped fresh
  mint or 1 teaspoon dried
Salt and pepper
⅓ cup milk
4 large pita breads, cut in
  half
½ cup chopped fresh parsley
¾ cup finely chopped scallions, with part of the
  green
1½ cups plain thick yogurt,
  at room temperature
¾ cup chopped cucumber

In a large bowl, combine the meat with the onions, bread crumbs, seasonings, and milk. Mix lightly until well blended. Moisten your hands and form the mixture into 32 sausage-shaped patties, about 2 inches long and ¾ inch in diameter. Grill over a white hot charcoal fire for 5 minutes on each side. Or bake in the oven on a baking sheet for 20 minutes at 350° F. Turn to brown evenly. Do not overcook. Drain off all the fat.

To serve, place 4 kofta in each pita pocket half. Top with the parsley, chopped scallions, and then a spoonful of yogurt. Chopped cucumber goes on the top. This gives the sandwich an interesting mixture of tastes and textures.

Argentinian Sausage Rolls

In this recipe, long thin chorizos rather than the short, fat ones work better. If you can only get the squat variety, cut them in half after they have been broiled.

6 Spanish or Portuguese
   chorizos (about 1½
   pounds)
2 large onions, chopped
1 large green pepper,
   chopped
2 garlic cloves, minced
Spanish paprika (available in
   Hispanic stores)
6 Italian hero rolls

Broil the chorizos until they are half-done, about 5 minutes, turning them often. Or brown them in a skillet for the same length of time. Remove and cut in half, if necessary. Reserve 2 tablespoon of the fat.

Sauté the onions, pepper, and garlic in the reserved fat. Do not brown. Add the half-cooked chorizos and season to taste with paprika; do not stint on the paprika.

Slice the rolls lengthwise and heat them for 5 minutes in a 250° F. oven. Fill each roll with a chorizo and some vegetables. Wrap in aluminum foil to keep them hot. The sandwich should be eaten from the wrapper. Just expose a bit and bite.

Smoked Sausage Sandwich

Yield: 8 sandwiches

Polish vendors offer this tasty sandwich. The more garlicky the kielbasa, the more tantalizing the aroma.

2 tablespoons butter
1 cup chopped onion
1 green pepper, cut in thin strips
1½ pounds kielbasa, cut in ¼-inch slices
2 cups well-drained sauerkraut
2 tablespoons prepared Dijon-style mustard
1 cup sour cream
8 French rolls, each about 8 inches long
Shredded lettuce

In a large skillet, melt the butter. Add the onion and green pepper and sauté until tender, about 5 minutes. Add the sausages and sauté a few more minutes, until they are lightly browned. Drain off all the fat. Add the sauerkraut to the pan and combine with the sausage mixture. Combine the mustard and sour cream and add to the mixture. Stir and cook over low heat until heated through but not boiling.

Slice the rolls lengthwise and remove a little of the center. Spoon some of the mixture into bottom half of each roll. Top with shredded lettuce. Place the top of each roll over the lettuce and press down slightly.

This is wonderful picnic fare. Bring a bottle of red wine and don't forget the napkins.

Heroes

As a wise man once said, "Health food may be good for the conscience, but heroes taste a hell of a lot better."

It is not clear where this sandwich originated. New York, San Francisco, and Baltimore, among other places, claim to have sired it. For obvious reasons, a vendor will not let you prepare your own. But when served at home, it really is a delightful meal. Just put out all the fixings and let people help themselves. You can add or subtract from the assortment, but all meat and cheese should be very thinly sliced.

Street vendors also call these monsters hoagies, submarines, torpedoes, grinders, and probably a few other things. I like to think of these sandwiches as heroes. You are a real hero if the sandwich you create is so courageous that you cannot get your mouth around it. A half-hero concocts an unadventurous sandwich. A coward just settles for the familiar lettuce, tomatoes, and Swiss cheese.

8 large French rolls, 6 inches long and 3 inches wide
Olive oil
Oregano
¼ pound pepperoni, thinly sliced
¼ pound boiled ham, thinly sliced
¼ pound Italian salami, thinly sliced
¼ pound mortadella, thinly sliced
¼ pound provolone, thinly sliced
¼ pound Swiss cheese, thinly sliced
1 onion, sliced in thin rounds
2 tomatoes, thinly sliced
Italian pepper relish (available in most supermarkets)
Shredded lettuce
Mustard
Mayonnaise
Butter

Cut each roll in half. To make a hero, scoop out a little of the bread from one of the rolls. Drizzle olive oil and oregano on one half. Begin piling on the meat, cheese, onion, tomatoes, pepper relish, and shredded lettuce until the sandwich reaches heroic proportions. Dress the other half of the roll with mustard, mayonnaise, or butter and set on top of the hero. Repeat with the remaining rolls and fillings.

Serve with olives and pickle slices. Marinated vegetables also make a good accompaniment.

Meatball Heroes

This sandwich is particularly popular at street fairs. In New York, the feast of San Gennaro would not be the same without these Italian heroes.

1 pound lean ground beef
½ cup finely chopped onion
1 garlic clove, minced
¼ cup water
½ teaspoon dried oregano
1 teaspoon salt
½ teaspoon black pepper
½ cup dry fine bread
   crumbs
1 tablespoon olive oil
2 medium-size peppers
   (green or red), seeded and
   coarsely chopped
1 (15-ounce) jar spaghetti
   sauce or 2 cups homemade
   sauce
4 Italian hero rolls, about 6
   inches long
Grated Parmesan cheese
Dried crushed red pepper
   (optional)

Mix together the meat, onion, garlic, water, seasonings, and bread crumbs. Shape into 12 meatballs about 1½ inches in diameter.

In a skillet, heat the olive oil. Add the meatballs and sauté until browned. Remove the meatballs and set them aside. Add the peppers to the drippings in the skillet and sauté for 3 minutes. Drain off the excess fat. Return the meatballs to skillet along with the spaghetti sauce. Cover and simmer for 15 minutes.

Heat the rolls for 5 minutes at 250° F. and slice them lengthwise about halfway down, taking care not to cut the roll through. Place 3 meatballs on each roll and spoon some sauce over them. Top with the cheese and red pepper.

These should be wrapped in a paper napkin and eaten with an extra paper napkin in hand.

Sausage Heroes

One sausage per sandwich is enough hero for most people. Some vendors serve 2 (or maybe 3). The sandwiches you buy on the street are usually made with hot Italian sausages, the hotter the better. If you can't stand the pain, sweet sausages can be substituted.

4 Italian-style sausages (hot or sweet)
1 tablespoon oil
3 onions, coarsely chopped
2 large green peppers, coarsely chopped
Salt and pepper
4 Italian hero rolls, about 6 inches long

Place the sausages in a cold skillet and cook over medium-high heat until they are cooked through and browned. Or grill on a charcoal grill until cooked through and browned.

In another skillet, heat the oil, add the onions and peppers, and sauté until the onions are limp and golden and the peppers are brown, but still a little crisp. Add salt and pepper to taste.

Slice the rolls lengthwise without cutting them through. Place a sausage on each roll and cover with onion-pepper mixture. Serve at once.

Lamb-Filled Gyros

Yield: 8 gyros

Gyro (rhymes with hero) means round-and-round in Greek. On warm evenings, in virtually every town throughout Greece, street vendors appear with their vertical round rotisseries. What makes the best gyro? Beef or lamb? Should the meat be slivered or ground? Such delicious controversies!

For these Greek-style pita sandwiches, the best way to barbecue the lamb is on a vertical rotisserie, but marinating the meat and quickly sautéing it is almost as good.

¼ cup lemon juice
½ cup olive oil (Greek, if possible)
3 garlic cloves, minced
3 tablespoons fresh mint or 2 teaspoons dried
3 tablespoons fresh oregano or 2 teaspoons dried
2 pounds lamb from the leg or the loin, thinly sliced
2 cups thick unflavored yogurt (Greek style, if possible)
1 large cucumber, peeled and chopped
1 garlic clove, finely minced
2 tablespoons chopped fresh dill
2 tablespoons red wine vinegar
2 tablespoons olive oil
4 large pita breads
2 cups shredded lettuce
½ cup finely chopped onion
1 large tomato, sliced
½ cup feta cheese, crumbled

Mix together the lemon juice, ½ cup olive oil, 3 garlic cloves, mint, and oregano. Place the sliced meat in the mixture and marinate for 3 to 4 hours at room temperature, or overnight in the refrigerator.

Combine the yogurt with the cucumber, 1 garlic clove, dill, and vinegar. This sauce is called tzatziki. Refrigerate until ready to use.

Remove the lamb from the marinade. Remove the tzatziki from the refrigerator and bring to room temperature. Heat the remaining 2 tablespoons olive oil in a skillet, add the lamb, and lightly sauté for 5 minutes. The lamb should not be overcooked.

Warm the pita breads in a 250° F. oven for 5 minutes. Slice in half. Pack some sautéed lamb into each pita pocket. Top with the shredded lettuce, onion, and tomato. Spoon some sauce on top. Crumble the feta cheese over the sauce and serve.

Beef-Filled Gyros

¼ cup red wine vinegar
3 tablespoons olive oil
2 garlic cloves, minced
3 tablespoons fresh oregano
   or 1 teaspoon dried
2 tablespoons fresh thyme or
   ½ teaspoon dried
Salt and pepper
2 pounds boneless sirloin
   steak, slivered
1 tablespoon butter
4 large pita breads, halved
1 cup diced tomatoes
1 cup diced cucumber
3 scallions, including some
   of the green part, chopped
3 tablespoons fresh chopped
   chives or 1 teaspoon dried
2 tablespoons fresh chopped
   dill or 1 teaspoon dried
1 cup thick sour cream (or
   part yogurt)
3 cups shredded lettuce
½ cup crumbled feta cheese

In a bowl, combine the vinegar, oil, garlic, oregano, thyme, and salt and pepper to taste for the marinade. Add the steak and marinate for several hours at room temperature. Remove the meat from the marinade and drain.

Heat the butter in a skillet until bubbly, add the meat and sauté for a few minutes until the meat browns. Place some of the steak in each pita pocket.

Combine the tomatoes, cucumber, scallions, chives, dill, and sour cream. Spoon over the meat. Top with shredded lettuce and crumbled feta and serve.

Hot Dogs:
From Frankfurt to Coney Island

The hot dog started out as a frankfurter. In Germany, in 1852, an inventive butcher spiced and smoked some sausages, and to honor his pet dog, he packed it into a casing shaped like a dachshund. The name of the dog is lost but the city of Frankfurt, where this momentous event occurred, has become immortalized.

In 1867, the frankfurter was brought to Coney Island in Brooklyn, New York, by Charles Feltman. His sausages were much in demand as street food, but his big problem was keeping them hot. As soon as he thought of using a small charcoal stove, he was in business. The frankfurter became the hot dog, and Coney Island became its spiritual home.

In 1916, Nathan's Hot Dog Stand in Coney Island put the hot dog into the gastronomic major leagues, though not without some fancy hype. Coney Island was then the watering place of high society. The rich who walked the boardwalk couldn't believe that anything that cost just a nickel could be good.

Long before it became the accepted way of business, Nathan did a bit of impromptu PR. He hired a few robust young men, dressed them in white coats, and staked them out in front of his stand. All they had to do was scarf down hot dogs and make a big to-do about how good they were. "Look," observed the high society types, "the doctors are eating them; they must be good." This was probably the first "doctors' endorsement."

The crowds came; Nathan became rich and famous. Kings and presidents and notables of the world have endorsed this sultan of street foods. Hot dogs have become an inevitable part of the country's national sport. It's hard to imagine a baseball game without the hot dog vendor hollering in the stands, "Get them while they're hot."

Purists insist that there is one way to eat a hot dog: wrapped in a proper hot dog bun with a thick ribbon of spicy mustard along its full length. The only permitted addition is warm sauerkraut. The onion and relish faction present a persuasive argument, but the unconvinced insist that though another presentation may taste good, it is not a real hot dog.

Best grilled over a charcoal fire just before they are popped into a warm roll, they can also be boiled. Hot dogs cannot be overcooked; they are a dependable, mouth-watering, foolproof food, no matter how inept the cook.

Texas Chili Dogs

A delicious evolution occurred when the hot dog acquired a Tex-Mex flavor. In spite of the protestations of those who lobby for the uncorrupted hot dog, the chili dog has now become a popular street food throughout America. There are two chili-dog schools: the chili dog with beans and the chili dog without. In this recipe the beans can be omitted if you feel strongly about it.

2 tablespoons oil
1 large onion, chopped
2 garlic cloves, chopped
½ pound lean ground beef
1 (15-ounce) can Italian-style
   chopped tomatoes,
   drained
1 (15-ounce) can chili beans
1 tablespoon chili powder or
   to taste
Salt and pepper
6 hot dogs
6 hot dog buns
Chopped raw onion
   (optional)

In a skillet, heat the oil, add the onion and garlic, and sauté for 5 minutes. Add the beef and sauté until brown. Add the tomatoes, beans, chili powder, and salt and pepper to taste. Cover and simmer for 10 minutes. Add the hot dogs and simmer for another 5 minutes to heat them through. Partially fill each roll with the beef-chili mixture. Place a hot dog on top. Top with additional chopped raw onion, if desired, and serve.

European Workman's Sandwich

Before this came to be known as a workman's sandwich, it was probably an "eat-what's-there" meal for the man who needed a protein fix in the middle of the day.

These combinations cross ethnic lines. All you need are meat and cheese that complement each other. Allow ¼ pound of meat and cheese for each sandwich. Hard French rolls work well for most of these combinations, but other ethnic breads are even better. French, English, or German mustards add a little more zing. Dill pickles, gherkins, mustard pickles, or hot cherry pickles are natural accompaniments.

Suggested Combinations

Polish kielbasa and Danish havarti

Lebanon bologna and Jarlsberg Swiss

German cervelat and Muenster (or tilsit)

Braunschweiger liver sausage and Gruyère

Spanish chorizo and manchego

Smoked pork and Dutch Gouda

Danish smoked salami and danbo

Italian soft salami and fontina

English ham and Gloucester

Slit open Italian or French bread cut into 6-inch lengths. Butter or not, depending on taste. Pile on the meat and cheese combination of your choice. Cover with the other half of the bread.

This is wonderful picnic fare. Bring along the mustard and pickles. A jug of red wine makes a perfect accompaniment.

Pan Bagnat

Yield: 4 sandwiches

As far back as anyone can remember, this unique sandwich has been served from carts along the beaches of Nice on the French Riviera. Originally, a pan bagnat was nothing more than a salade Niçoise served in a small round loaf of bread. In Nice, there is even a special bread baked for this local delicacy, but any crusty round loaf, about 8 inches across, will do.

By now, the pan bagnat has traveled around the world and innovators have had their way with this worthy sandwich. Some of the newer versions may provide delicious additions and substitutions, but they are not the real thing.

Advocates of true Niçoise cookery would never use any cooked vegetable in either salade Niçoise or pan bagnat. There is even a ritual about the tomatoes. They must be quartered (never sliced), salted 3 times, and moistened with olive oil. You can leave out 1 or 2 ingredients and still have an authentic pan bagnat. The only "must" is the olives.

In Nice, the pan bagnat is eaten by the local population as a mid-morning snack, served about 9 o'clock to early risers. But it can be eaten at any time. It is superb picnic fare and a glorious meal in itself.

Vinaigrette

3 tablespoons red wine
  vinegar
½ cup olive oil
1 tablespoon capers
5 anchovies, drained and
  pureed or mashed
½ teaspoon dried thyme
Salt and pepper to taste

Sandwich

4 round crusty French bread
  rolls
2 large garlic cloves, minced
½ cup black olives (Niçoise,
  dry, oil-cured Italian, or
  Greek), pitted and
  flattened
1 large beefsteak tomato, cut
  into small wedges
1 (7½-ounce) can tuna
  (Italian, preferably),
  packed in oil, drained and
  flaked
3 hard-boiled eggs, sliced
1 large Spanish (or red)
  onion, sliced very thin
1 large green pepper, seeded
  and julienned
1 large red pepper, seeded
  and julienned
1 large cucumber, very
  thinly sliced
Finely chopped fresh basil

First, blend all the ingredients for the vinaigrette. Set aside.

Halve the rolls. Scoop out some of the white part. Rub the cut sides of the rolls with garlic. Brush the rolls generously with the vinaigrette. Divide all the ingredients among the roll halves, drizzling some of the vinaigrette on the tuna and tomatoes. Sprinkle with basil. Top with the remaining halves of bread. Weight the sandwiches with a heavy plate for about an hour to blend the flavors.

Serve with chilled white wine.

Falafel

Yield: 6 sandwiches

Falafel is an ancient dish that started in the Arabian peninsula. It was first brought to Israel by the Jews of Yemen. Egyptians and Syrians have their own versions of falafel, but Israel claims it as their national dish. There is even in Tel Aviv a self-anointed king of falafel whose kiosk proclaims his royalty and avows that his falafel is the ultimate street food.

1 cup raw fine bulgur (crushed wheat)
1 (1-pound) can chick-peas, drained
1 large onion, chopped
2 garlic cloves, chopped
2 tablespoons finely chopped fresh parsley
1 egg, slightly beaten
1 teaspoon salt
1 teaspoon dried hot red peppers, ground or very finely chopped (optional)
2 teaspoons ground cumin
1 teaspoon ground coriander
3 to 4 tablespoons flour
Oil for deep frying
3 large pita breads, cut in half
Tahina sauce
Chopped tomatoes
Chopped onions
Chopped cucumbers
Sliced radishes

First, prepare the Tahina Sauce (below) and set it aside.

Cover the bulgur with boiling water. Cover the bowl and set aside for about 30 minutes, until the bulgur softens. Drain thoroughly.

In a food processor or blender, combine the chick-peas with the onion, garlic, parsley, egg, salt, red peppers, cumin, coriander, and flour. Process for 1 minute, until the mixture is well blended. Do not overprocess or the mixture will liquefy.

Add enough bulgur so that the mixture forms a ball without sticking to your hands; it should be thick. If it is too loose, add a little more flour. Form the mixture into small balls about the size of a quarter and flatten them slightly.

Preheat the oil to 365° F. and deep fry the chick-pea balls until golden brown. Do not let them darken or the falafel will be dry. Drain on paper towels and serve them hot in pita bread (several in each sandwich) topped with Tahina Sauce and chopped tomato, onion, cucumber, and radishes.

Tahina Sauce

1 cup tahina (sesame seed paste)
3 garlic cloves, chopped
1 teaspoon salt
½ cup finely chopped fresh parsley
¼ cup finely chopped fresh mint (optional)
¾ cup fresh lemon juice

Combine the tahina, garlic, salt, parsley, and mint in food processor or blender. Process until combined. Add the lemon juice slowly in a steady stream until the mixture has the consistency of mayonnaise. Add a little more lemon juice or water to get the correct consistency. Spoon on top of the falafel in the pita bread.

46

Street Food

Cuban Sandwich

This sandwich goes back to the early 1900s, brought to Florida by the Cubans who fled to the U.S. during the Spanish-American War. It became a favorite street food in every Cuban community. In those days no one had even heard of cholesterol, and the common attitude was that if 2 meats were good, 3 were better. Smoked ham, fresh pork, and salami, along with Swiss cheese, make up this hearty sandwich.

1 French baguette
Soft butter for spreading
¼ pound cooked smoked ham, thinly sliced
¼ pound roast pork loin, thinly sliced
¼ pound salami, thinly sliced
¼ pound Swiss cheese, thinly sliced
Dijon-style mustard
Sour pickles

Slice the bread lengthwise; spread lightly with butter. Layer the smoked ham, fresh pork, salami, and Swiss cheese on half the bread. Spread the top half with mustard and cover the sandwich. Press down firmly and cut into 4 sandwiches. You can heat this sandwich to crisp the bread and blend the flavors. It is traditionally served with a sour pickle.

Roti Sandwich: A Caribbean Creation

In the Caribbean, roti is the generic name for a flat Indian bread. The roti was brought to the Caribbean when the Indians came to Trinidad as indentured servants to work on the sugar plantations. There were no lunch breaks and the field workers found it convenient to wrap their curries in bread and eat them when they could. The roti could be filled with curried anything: potatoes, pumpkin, chickpeas, chicken, goat, seafood.

Today roti stands are ubiquitous throughout the Caribbean. And the rotis are still filled with curried anything. The local custom dictates that the roti is eaten while walking. The stuffed pancake must not be removed from its wrapper; just expose a bit at a time, munch, and march.

A real aficionado will add additional curry-blend spices, offered by the vendor, to the already sizzling mixture. Caribbean spices, as one would expect from a region where so many cultures meet, is a blend of French, Spanish, African, and Indian. It is hard to sort out origins. Put it all together and you have a unique Creole mixture. Garlic is an important ingredient; chili peppers and lime juice play off each other. It is customary to ask that a bit of *amchar* be added to the roti before the bread envelope is folded; amchar is the tamarind paste that acts as a foil for the fiery curry.

Roti Pancakes

I would like to thank Dunstan Harris author of Island Cooking: Recipes from the Caribbean *(The Crossing Press), who so graciously shared this recipe with me; he made it sound so easy. This recipe makes an authentic roti bread but Indian paratha, which can be found in specialty shops, works very well for the fillings that follow as well.*

2 cups sifted all-purpose
  flour
¼ teaspoon baking soda
½ teaspoon salt
½ to ¾ cup milk
Vegetable oil for frying

Sift together the dry ingredients. Add enough milk to form a stiff dough. Knead on a well-floured board until the dough becomes elastic. Form the dough into 4 equal-size balls.

With a rolling pin, roll each ball flat to form a 12-inch circle. With a pastry brush, spread on a thin coating of vegetable oil. Form the dough into balls again; cover them with a towel and allow them to stand for 15 minutes at room temperature. Roll them out again into the same 12-inch circles and pat them lightly.

Heat a cast iron skillet or griddle over high heat, until a drop of water sizzles when dropped on it. Spread the skillet with a thin layer of oil and place one roti circle in the pan. Cook for 1 minute, flip, and spread the cooked surface with a thin layer of oil. Turn the roti every few minutes until it is cooked and brown flecks appear, about 5 minutes. Remove the roti from the skillet; let it cool for 1 minute. Then pound it between the palms of the hands until it becomes supple. Keep it warm and moist by covering it with a towel while cooking the other 3 roti.

Spicy Potato Rotis

1 pound baking potatoes
2 tablespoons vegetable oil
½ teaspoon mustard seeds
1 large sweet onion, chopped
½ teaspoon turmeric
½ teaspoon ground cumin
1 teaspoon hot chili powder
Salt and pepper
¼ cup finely chopped fresh
  cilantro (also known as
  fresh coriander and
  Chinese parsley)
4 roti pancakes (page 49)

Peel the potatoes and cut them into large chunks. Boil them in salted water to cover until they are slightly undercooked, about 5 minutes. Cut them into 1/2-inch cubes and set them aside.

Heat the oil in a large heavy skillet and fry the mustard seeds until they begin to pop. Add the onion and fry for 5 minutes, stirring occasionally, making sure that the pieces do not stick to the bottom of the pan. Add the remaining spices and salt and pepper to taste. Cook for a few more minutes, stirring constantly. Add the potatoes and cook for 5 minutes, stirring occasionally. Remove the mixture from the heat and add the cilantro.

Place a fourth of the mixture in the center of each roti and fold the bread around it like an envelope, tucking the ends underneath. Put each roti in an aluminum foil wrapper to keep it warm.

Trinidad Shrimp Curry Rotis

¾ teaspoon cumin seeds
¾ teaspoon coriander seeds
¾ teaspoon mustard seeds
½ teaspoon freshly ground
  pepper
¾ teaspoon turmeric
¼ teaspoon crushed hot red
  pepper
2 tablespoons vegetable oil
1 medium-size onion, finely
  chopped
1 large garlic clove, finely
  chopped
1 tablespoon finely chopped
  fresh ginger root
3 medium-size firm ripe
  tomatoes, peeled, seeded,
  and finely chopped
½ cup water
1 teaspoon salt
1 pound medium-size
  shrimp, shelled and
  deveined
2 tablespoons fresh lime
  juice
4 roti pancakes (page 49)

Combine all the spices in a blender or a food processor and blend at high speed until the spices are pulverized.

In a heavy skillet, heat the oil over moderate heat. Add the onion, garlic, and ginger and sauté, stirring frequently, until the onions are transparent, about 5 minutes. Do not let the mixture burn. Add the pulverized spices and stir for 2 minutes. Add the tomatoes, water, and salt and bring to a boil over high heat. Cook briskly until most of the liquid has evaporated, stirring frequently. The mixture should be thick.

Add the shrimp and stir the ingredients to coat them. Reduce the heat as low as possible, cover the skillet tightly, and simmer for about 5 minutes, until the shrimp are firm and pink. Remove from the heat and stir in the lime juice.

Place one fourth of the mixture in the center of each roti. Fold the bread around the filling like an envelope, tucking the ends underneath. Place each roti in an aluminum foil wrapper to keep it warm.

Hot Cauliflower Rotis

2 tablespoons vegetable oil
1 tablespoon finely chopped fresh ginger root
1 garlic clove, finely chopped
1 medium-size onion, finely chopped
1 teaspoon turmeric
⅛ teaspoon ground red pepper
1 medium-size cauliflower (about 1 pound), finely chopped
1 tablespoon finely chopped hot green chili
1 teaspoon ground cumin
1 teaspoon salt
4 roti pancakes (page 49)

In a heavy skillet over high heat, heat the oil until it is almost smoking. Stir in the ginger root and garlic; then stir in the onions. Lower the heat to moderate and fry the mixture for about 5 minutes, stirring occasionally, until the onions are golden brown. Do not allow the onions to burn.

Stir in the turmeric, red pepper, cauliflower, chili, cumin, and salt. Cover the skillet, reduce the heat to low, and cook for about 10 minutes, until the cauliflower is tender.

Remove from the heat and place one fourth of the mixture in the center of each roti. Fold the bread around it like an envelope, tucking the ends underneath. Place each roti in an aluminum foil wrapper to keep it warm.

Philadelphia Cheese Steak

Yield: 4 sandwiches

Philadelphians boast that their city has given to the world of street food the perfect cheese-steak sandwich, which is no minor accomplishment when you consider its humble ingredients: thinly sliced beef, provolone or American cheese, fried onions — nothing fancy. (Some devotees claim that frozen sandwich steak, such as Steakums, and Cheez Whiz, makes the best of all cheese steak sandwiches.) Traditionally, this sandwich is eaten while standing up, not very far from the vendor.

1 pound beef sirloin
4 French or Italian rolls,
   about 6 inches in length
2 tablespoons vegetable oil
2 large onions, very thinly
   sliced
Salt and black pepper
4 slices American or
   provolone cheese
Pickled hot cherry peppers

Slice the meat very thin. A good way to do this is to partially freeze the meat before slicing.

Warm the rolls in a 250° F. oven for about 5 minutes.

In a heavy skillet, heat the oil, add the steak and quickly fry until it is just brown; do not overcook. Remove the steak from the pan. Add the onions to the pan and sauté until lightly brown, adding a bit more oil if necessary. Season with salt and pepper to taste.

Slice the warmed rolls in half lengthwise. Place the steak slices on the bottom half of the rolls. Top with the onions and 1 cheese slice. Top with the other half of the roll. The cheese should just begin to melt.

Serve immediately with cherry peppers.

Baltimore Crab Cakes

If you can make this sandwich during crabbing season when the crab meat is at its most succulent, you are in for a bit of gustatory heaven. Frozen crab meat is a good substitute, if you don't compare it to the just-off-the-boat crab meat flavor. It's not worth the effort to use imitation crab meat.

The traditional way of serving these crab cakes is on saltine crackers. If you prefer to use crackers rather than toasted hamburger buns, make the crab cakes a little smaller.

1 pound crab meat
Fresh bread crumbs made from 2 slices white bread
½ cup milk
1½ teaspoons Dijon-style mustard
½ teaspoon white pepper
1 tablespoon Worcestershire sauce
Salt
2 egg yolks
1 tablespoon mayonnaise
1 tablespoon chopped fresh parsley
1 cup flour
1 egg beaten with 1 tablespoon water
½ cup dry bread crumbs
3 tablespoons vegetable oil
4 to 6 hamburger buns or soft rolls, toasted, or 12 large saltine crackers

Pick over the crab meat to remove any bits of shell and cartilage.

Mix together the fresh bread crumbs and milk; squeeze to remove excess milk. Combine the bread crumbs, crab meat, mustard, pepper, Worcestershire sauce, and salt to taste. Add the egg yolks, mayonnaise, and parsley and combine thoroughly. The mixture should hold together.

Form the mixture into 4 to 6 large flat cakes. Coat the crab cakes with flour, dip into the egg-water mixture and then roll in the dry bread crumbs.

Heat the oil in a skillet to 375° F. Add the crab cakes and fry until brown on both sides. Drain them on paper towels. Serve immediately on toasted buns.

Although vendors do not usually supply an accompanying beverage, when served at home, a glass of chilled dry white wine makes this sandwich even more special.

Croque Monsieur

The French verb croquer *means to munch, and, of course,* monsieur *means gentleman. Does this rather whimsical name mean to munch the gentleman, or a gentleman-sized munch?*

There are many versions of the croque monsieur *found throughout France. This is the one you are likely to find in Paris.*

8 slices firm-textured white
    bread
16 thin slices good-quality
    Gruyère cheese
8 slices smoked ham
6 tablespoons clarified butter
Cornichons (small French
    gherkins)

Top 4 slices of the bread with 1 slice of cheese, 1 slice of ham, and another slice of cheese. Cover with the other bread slices. (You can trim the crust from the bread, if you like). Press the sandwiches down firmly. Brush the tops of the sandwiches with clarified butter.

Coat a large heavy flat-bottomed skillet with clarified butter. Heat the skillet until the butter just begins to bubble. Place the sandwiches in the skillet, buttered side down, and fry slowly over medium heat.

Brush the tops of sandwiches with additional clarified butter. Turn when golden brown and cook for additional 3 to 4 minutes until golden on the other side. Serve immediately with cornichons. Cherry tomatoes marinated in a basil dressing is a perfect accompaniment. Together they make a luscious lunch.

Note: To clarify butter, melt butter in a small saucepan and skim the foam from the top. Pour the clear melted (clarified) butter into another pan. Discard the milky residue in the first pan.

Sandwich Innovations

It is not clear how or where bagels began. They seem to have started in Vienna as *bügel*, which is the old German word for ring. They made their way to Poland, where they were used as teething rings after they became stale and hard. By the time they got to Russia, they were called *bubliki* and invested with magical powers, as were many circular objects.

Bagels came to America with the Jewish immigrants and for at least 50 years were popular only in Jewish neighborhoods. In New York City, a stop at the local bakery to pick up warm fragrant bagels—plain, poppy seed, or egg—was an unvarying part of the Sunday morning ritual. It took a person of Spartan fortitude to deliver all the bagels intact. Most families permitted one big bite en route.

The bagels were picked up after a visit to the appetizing store. It was common knowledge in Jewish neighborhoods in New York City that all appetizing foods came from an "appetizing store." The display of foods—about 20 kinds of smoked fish, olives of all sizes, both black and green, pickles in various stages of sourness swimming in garlicky brine, large tubs of halvah in three flavors, toasted pine nuts in the shell known as Indian nuts, dried apricot "shoe leather," and other exotic sweets—was almost more than the eye could manage. This vision was joined by a concourse of fragrance that enveloped one at the door. Closing your eyes, inhaling deeply, and sighing became almost an involuntary act.

Lox (smoked salmon) was the favored smoked fish. Lox and fresh cream cheese, cut from a large loaf, were always served on bagels. The approved way of eating a bagel sandwich was to cut the warm bagel in half and fill it with a thick layer of cream cheese topped with slices of lox. A bit of thinly sliced onion and a squirt of fresh lemon juice were lovely embellishments, but not really necessary.

Bagels now come in flavors unheard of 20 years ago. Old bagel-lovers will have nothing to do with cinnamon and raisin bagels or chili-flavored bagels, and who ever heard of pizza bagels? But people who are not burdened with tradition love them. Vendors have taken the original bagel and all its innovations into the street; their carts sport names such as "Bagel-o-rama" and "Bagel Mania." Bagels have gained such international acceptance they have even been sighted in China.

Like the bagel, the croissant is a recent entry in the street food marketplace. For hundreds of years, *le petit dejeuner* of croissant and *café au lait* has sustained the French throughout the morning. But, the croissant didn't start out as a street food. In fact, it isn't even French.

The story goes that in 1686 the Turks were besieging Budapest. To reach the center of the city, they dug underground tunnels. But bakers, who were working through the night, heard the noise and alerted the troops; the city was saved. As a reward, the bakers were given the privilege of baking a special pastry in the shape of a crescent, the emblem of the Ottoman flag.

If this bit of history has a familiar ring, it is the same story, almost word for word, that was told about the pretzel bakers who saved Vienna in 1529. Could the rulers of the Ottoman Empire have made the same dumb mistake twice? Such slow learners!

The croissant is the ultimate roll. Anyone who has ever enjoyed a croissant in France has that experience stored in culinary memory. Even the simplest fare is enhanced when it is served in a rich, butter-laden croissant, still warm from the bakery. Suddenly ham and cheese, egg salad, sliced turkey become elegant edibles.

"Melts" are now offered as street food; the only special equipment needed is a broiler. In California, where the melt began, the word means melted cheese. The cheese used is usually Monterey jack because it melts so smoothly, though other melting cheeses work equally well. Crab, tuna, beef patty, sausage, even avocado slices, topped with cheese, make delicious melts. Any bread or roll provides a suitable base; the bagel melt adds a chewy texture that makes the sandwich something special.

Hamburger Melt

¾ pound lean ground beef
Salt and pepper
1 teaspoon vegetable oil
2 large onions, thinly sliced
2 large bagels, sliced in half
4 slices Monterey jack cheese
½ tablespoon butter

Combine the beef and salt and pepper to taste and form into 4 flat patties. Grill in a heavy skillet over medium-high heat for 3 to 4 minutes on each side. Remove from the pan. Add the oil and heat. Then add the onions and sauté until golden brown.

Lightly butter the outside of the halved bagels. Arrange the sautéed onions and beef patties (in that order) on the bagel halves. Top with the cheese. Place on a hot griddle for 2 minutes, until warmed through. Transfer to a broiler and heat just until the cheese melts. Do not let it burn.

A variation of this is to use a whole bagel for each sandwich. After you top the patty with cheese, cover with the other half of the bagel and toast on the griddle for 2 to 3 minutes, cheese side down, until the cheese melts.

Stuffed and Savory

A milestone in culinary evolution occurred at the beginning of civilization when someone thought to combine meal and water and cook it on a hot stone. From that inauspicious beginning, the pancake arose.

It is lost to history who first thought of the refinement of stuffing delicious morsels into a pancake or a pastry pocket, but almost every ethnic group does it. The Mexican taco, the English savory pie, the Argentine empanada, the Italian pizza, samosas in India, the Chinese spring roll, the French crêpe are all elaborations of the original pancake.

The unique features of the various pancakes are shaped by the culture in which they evolved and how they migrated from one area to another. Although no one could mistake a Mexican tortilla for a Chinese spring roll wrapper, it is impossible to trace the history of any one wrapper, or figure out who is responsible for what.

A good example is the tortilla. We know that Mexican food has Aztec, and to a lesser extent, Mayan origins. These are interwoven with the cuisines of Spain and Portugal, which in turn were dominated by Arab (Middle Eastern) influences.

For thousands of years, making tortillas was entrusted to the women of the village. Girls learned from their mothers how to clap and slap the native ground masa harina into flat pancakes and bake them on an improvised griddle. Their original recipes are very similar to what we use today. Flour tortillas came later; but in the north of Mexico, they have almost replaced the corn tortilla.

Today, tortilla making is a dying art because neatly packaged tortillas are now available even in remote Mexican villages. There is no need to make them at home unless you really enjoy clapping and slapping.

Those who lament that Mexican children will no longer learn this skill at home to pass on to their children should save some sympathy for Oriental children as well. Spring roll wrappers are now available in various sizes and shapes almost everywhere. This makes it easy to prepare the spring rolls, lumpias, and dumplings at home without having to deal with the vagaries of the dough wrappers. The popularity of these packaged skins throughout the Orient proves that even the most dedicated cooks often take this shortcut.

Just a few words about pizza dough. It can be argued that pizza has to be baked on the brick floor of a wood-burning bread oven for it to have the right flavor. That's the way it started in Italy.

Getting the pizza onto the floor of a hot oven was an acquired skill, best taught on the job in the family bakery. One can only imagine the verbal and hand exchanges between the master baker (father) and the inept apprentice (son) as the luckless youth managed to dump the dough on his shoes yet another time. A long-handled peel (baker's shovel) was used to slide it in and out of the oven. One gave it a twist of the wrist and jerked it off the peel; it was all in the wrist. Of course, you could never get the same result baking pizza in a pan in a regular oven.

Making a pizza dough from scratch is very satisfying and it is not nearly as complicated as it sounds. Using a pizza stone for baking gives the dough a slightly more authentic texture; however, the ordinary pizza lover can get excellent results with an ordinary pizza pan. But, if the thought of making a pizza crust from scratch seems overwhelming, check any supermarket for help. Like the tortilla and the spring roll wrapper, one never has to make a pizza dough unless one has the time and the desire to do it.

Mexican Snacks: Take a Taco

The tortilla is the basic ingredient of much Mexican-style street food. Tortillas can be rolled, stacked, or crumbled as chips. They can be stuffed, folded, baked, fried, sauced. Tacos, burritos, tostadas, enchiladas, chimichangas, to say nothing of flautas, chalupas, and quesadillas all begin with this versatile corn or flour pancake.

The fillings are a combination of meat and beans and cheese, plus what is in the local market. The chile pepper in its many forms adds zing and variety. Peppers range in hotness from the mild Anaheim pepper to the popular jalapeño and serrano peppers. The super fiery pequin is an acquired taste; you have to build up to it or be born Mexican. A useful bit of information about chili peppers is that usually the smaller the pepper, the hotter it is.

The American Tex-Mex and Cal-Mex variations are now part of our national cuisine. As one would expect, the street foods of Texas and California have incorporated the tastes of the large Mexican populations of those states.

Tacos have become one of the most enduring street foods. They are now enjoyed all over the world, including Paris. In Mexico, tacos are made of small 4-inch tortillas. They are usually rolled, shaped like an envelope, and then fried for a few minutes so they are warm but not crisp. If you want to eat a taco in true Mexican fashion, it

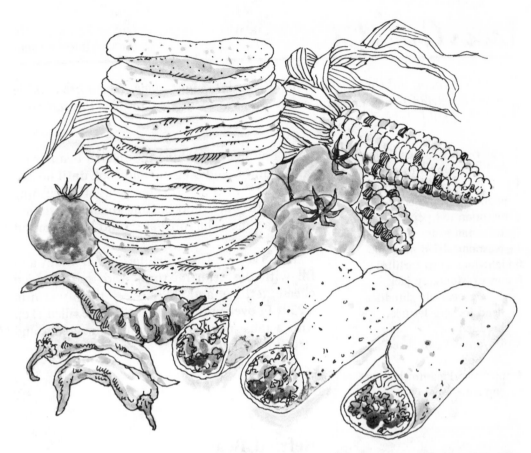

takes a little practice. As you tip one end of the taco to your mouth, you roll the other end with your finger so that none of the sauce is lost. In the U.S. the familiar U-shape tortilla that fits so comfortably in the hand is larger, 6 inches or 8 inches in diameter.

Taco fillings can be made of ground beef, or refried beans, or a combination of both. Toppings include guaca-mole, salsa (hot or mild), sour cream, shredded lettuce, grated cheese, chopped olives, or any blend of these ingredients. The fillings can be customized by adjusting the spices. If you prefer painless eating, go easy on the chili seasoning. If you enjoy eating and clearing your sinuses at the same time, add more of the fiery stuff.

Tacos Grandes

Yield: 6 tacos

These large tacos make a satisfying lunch or a late night snack. If you are making your own refried beans and the salsa, prepare them first to give the flavors a chance to blend.

2 cups Refried Beans (below)
    or 1 (15-ounce) can
1 to 2 dried red chili
    peppers, crumbled, or 1
    teaspoon red pepper flakes
½ teaspoon ground cumin
¼ teaspoon dried oregano
6 eight-inch corn tortillas
6 ounces Monterey jack
    cheese, coarsely shredded
½ head iceberg lettuce,
    shredded
1 (6¼-ounce) can sliced
    black olives
1 cup Salsa Picante (below)
½ cup sour cream

Over low heat, combine the refried beans with chili, cumin, and oregano and cook until heated through. Warm the tortillas by lightly brushing them with water and heating them in a skillet, one at a time. The tortillas should be warm but pliable.

To serve, hold the tortilla in your hand and fill with the bean mixture. Add the shredded cheese, lettuce, and olives. Keep them warm in a 250° F. oven until all the tortillas are filled. Top with a tablespoon of salsa and sour cream and serve immediately.

Refried Beans

2 cups dry red or pinto
    beans
2 teaspoons salt
1 tablespoon oil or lard
2 garlic cloves, finely
    chopped
1 medium-size onion,
    chopped
½ teaspoon ground cumin
½ teaspoon dried cilantro
    (fresh coriander or
    Chinese parsley)
Salt and pepper

Wash the beans and place them in a bowl. Add water to cover and the salt. Soak them overnight. Drain well. Place the soaked beans in a large saucepan, add water 1 inch over the top of the beans. Bring to a boil and cover. Cook slowly for 1 to 2 hours, until the beans are tender. Drain well, reserving 1 cup of the cooking water.

If you forget to soak the beans overnight, place them in a large saucepan and add water until the beans are covered by 1 inch of water. Add the salt. Cover and bring to a boil. Turn off the heat and allow the beans to sit, covered, for 1 hour. Drain and then add water and cook as above, until the beans are tender. Drain well, reserving 1 cup of the cooking water.

Heat the oil in a heavy skillet. Add the garlic and onion and cook until limp. Add the cumin,

Street Food

coriander, cooked beans, and 1 cup of the cooking water. When most of the water has evaporated, remove from the heat. Mash the beans well with a potato masher and add salt and pepper to taste. Makes 4 cups.

These beans can be frozen. Bring to room temperature before using.

Salsa Picante

½ cup fresh cilantro leaves
  (fresh coriander or
  Chinese parsley)
1 large garlic clove
2 medium-size tomatoes,
  quartered
1 medium-size onion,
  quartered
1 to 2 serrano peppers,
  halved and seeded
3 tablespoons tomato paste
1 teaspoon red wine vinegar
½ teaspoon salt
¼ teaspoon sugar

Place the cilantro in a food processor fitted with a steel blade or in a blender. Process for a few seconds. With the machine running, add the garlic, tomatoes, onion, and peppers through the feeder tube and chop coarsely, about 5 on/off turns. Add the tomato paste, vinegar, salt, and sugar and give it a few more turns. It should have a chunky consistency. Place the salsa in a small bowl, cover, and refrigerate until ready to use. Let the salsa stand at room temperature for 30 minutes to allow the flavors to blend. Serve at room temperature.

Super Burritos

Refried beans and salsa can be bought in a supermarket, but making them from scratch in your kitchen adds to the flavor of this delicious burrito. If you are making your own refried beans or salsa (see pages 62 to 63), prepare them first to give the flavors a chance to blend.

A burrito can be fried before serving, which makes it a chimichanga. There are instructions on some packaged tortilla wrappers for baking chimichangas rather than frying them. After they are filled, secure them with toothpicks and bake in a 350° F. oven until they are heated through, about 10 minutes. It is not as authentic as the method below, but lower in fat.

½ pound chorizos, hot or mild
1 cup chopped onion
½ cup chopped green pepper
1 garlic clove, minced
3 cups Refried Beans (page 62)
1 teaspoon chili powder (optional)
6 flour tortillas, at least 7 inches in diameter (a large tortilla makes a neater burrito)
1 (4-ounce) can diced green chilies, drained
1 cup grated sharp cheddar
Salsa Picante (page 63 or use a bottled variety) (optional)
Sour cream (optional)

Place the chorizos in a cold skillet. Turn the heat to medium-high and sauté them for about 15 minutes, until brown. Drain on paper towels and crumble.

In a small amount of the chorizo drippings, sauté the onion, green pepper, and garlic until soft, about 5 minutes. Add the refried beans and chili powder and heat through, about 10 minutes. Combine with the chorizos.

Brush the tortillas lightly with water. Heat them briefly to soften, one at a time, in a skillet or on a griddle. Keep them warm in a 250° F. oven.

Place about ¾ cup of the bean mixture in the center of each tortilla. Top with ½ tablespoon diced chilies and grated cheese. Fold the tortilla so that the top and bottom overlap. Then fold the opposite sides so they meet.

Serve the burritos immediately, wrapped in a large napkin, with salsa and sour cream, if desired. A cold beer is a perfect complement.

Note: After folding, the burritos can be secured with toothpicks and crisp-fried. In a deep heavy skillet, heat 1 inch of vegetable oil to 375° F. and fry the filled tortillas for 1 minute on each side until crisp and golden brown.

Fish Fillet Burritos

Watching the progress of these burritos across the United States is watching a street food success in the making. They started in Mexico and were brought to San Diego. They have already been sighted in Los Angeles and as far east as Denver.

The salsa should be prepared before the burritos so that it can mellow for a while.

4 fresh corn tortillas
Flour
Salt and pepper
4 fish fillets (about 1 pound firm white-fleshed fish such as cod)
6 tablespoons oil for frying
2 scallions, finely chopped
1½ cups grated Monterey Jack cheese
2 cups coarsely chopped lettuce

Wrap the tortillas in aluminum foil and warm them in a 250° F. oven for 15 minutes. Combine the flour with the salt and pepper to taste, and sprinkle over the fillets.

Heat the oil in a large heavy skillet. Add the fish and fry until golden, about 10 minutes, flipping it once. Place a fillet in the center of each warm tortilla. Sprinkle with a few scallions, grated cheese, and chopped lettuce. Top with salsa and serve.

Salsa Ranchero

1 tablespoon vegetable oil
⅔ cup chopped onion
1½ tablespoons minced serrano (or other hot green) chile
2 medium-size tomatoes, peeled and chopped
½ cup tomato juice
1 teaspoon salt

Heat the oil in a saucepan. Add the onion and the chile and sauté until the onion is translucent, 3 to 4 minutes. Add the chopped tomatoes, tomato juice, and salt. Reduce the heat and simmer for 5 minutes. Place the salsa in a small bowl, cover, and refrigerate until ready to use. Let the salsa stand at room temperature for 30 minutes before serving to allow the flavors to blend.

Empanadas: A Latin Turnover

Empanadas are thought of as South American meat pies. Some food historians argue that they probably arose in the Middle East thousands of years ago and for centuries were carried by Sephardic Jews over a long tortuous route to Spain and Portugal and were brought to the western hemisphere by the conquistadors in the fifteenth century. Here is an example of an ancient food that goes back to early times and has survived almost intact. On twelfth-century Spanish cathedrals in Galicia there are stone statues holding empanadas almost identical to the turnovers sold today in the street markets of Central and South America.

Although all empanadas may have the same roots, they branch in different directions. In Central and South America, the indigenous corn is often utilized; in Spain and Portugal, wheat is used almost exclusively. The Mediterranean countries favor garlic; Mexicans and South Americans are chile enthusiasts.

Empanadas go by various names. They can be *empadas*, *empadinhas*, *empanaditas*, *empanadillas*. The name reveals the size of the turnover, and often the degree of affection one feels for the meat pie. Mama's *empanaditas* are always something special. In general, *empanadas* are larger than the diminutive *empadinhas*. In English they are called meat pies, hot pockets, or turnovers.

Wherever Latin-Americans congregate in the U.S., empanadas are a popular street food, but in Latin and South America, they are almost always appetizers, served as the first part of a meal. Although Argentina and Chile both claim to be the true home of the empanada in the western hemisphere, every country, every area in Central and South America has its variations. It is possible to start in Mexico City and work your way down to Buenos Aires sampling nothing but empanadas and never eating the same turnover twice.

Empanadas can be filled with almost any kind of meat or fish, singly or in combination. It's hard to tell from the outside what delicious mixture you will find on the inside. Like so many ethnic foods, empanadas are stuffed with what is most plentiful. Pork, chicken, shrimp, fresh sardines, lampreys are some of the foods found in empanadas, combined with onions, peppers, zucchini, celery, spinach. Olives, raisins, and hard-boiled eggs add flavor and textural variety.

Use your favorite spicy seasonings for your empanada fillings. Even if you find the ideal combination, chances are you will not be able to repeat it because you won't remember the exact proportions. The only important thing to remember is that fillings for empanadas should be firm so the pastry doesn't get soggy during baking.

Empanadas de Queso

Yield: About 30 empanadas

These deep-fried cheese turnovers are from Bolivia. If the filling seems too bland, add more seasonings to the cheese mixture.

½ pound cheddar cheese, grated
4 scallions, white and green parts, finely chopped
3 egg yolks, slightly beaten
Salt and white pepper
½ teaspoon paprika
1 teaspoon chili powder
½ teaspoon ground cumin
2½ cups sifted all-purpose flour
¼ cup melted butter or margarine
1 teaspoon salt
Approximately 1 cup lukewarm water
Oil for deep frying

Combine the cheese, scallions, egg yolks, and seasonings. Chill for 1 hour before using. The mixture should be stiff.

Mix together the flour, butter, salt, and enough water to make a soft dough. This can be done in the food processor. Divide the dough into 2 balls.

On a floured board, roll out each ball of dough until very thin. Using a 4-inch glass or cookie cutter, cut into circles. Place 1 tablespoon of the cheese mixture on each circle and fold over. Moisten the edges of the pastry with water and press the edges together firmly to seal.

Heat the oil to 375° F. and fry the empanadas, a few at a time, until golden brown, 3 to 4 minutes. Drain on paper towels and serve immediately.

Argentinian Empanadas

This is a classic dish, eaten throughout Argentina. It is not only a snack food, it is also a mainstay of people working in the field, since it can easily be eaten out of hand. Depending on the amount of seasonings, these empanadas can range from almost bland to tongue-searing. Don't omit the raisins; they are needed to absorb excess liquid while the empanadas are baking.

Pastry

2 cups all-purpose flour
½ cup finely ground cornmeal
1 teaspoon baking powder
½ teaspoon salt
¼ cup cold lard
¼ cup cold butter
2 large egg yolks
Cold water
1 egg beaten with ½ teaspoon water

Filling

1 tablespoon olive oil
¾ pound lean ground beef
2 garlic cloves, minced
1 medium-size onion, finely chopped
1 medium-size potato, cooked and diced
2 ripe tomatoes, peeled and chopped
1 fresh hot red pepper, finely chopped (optional)
Salt and pepper
1 teaspoon paprika
1 teaspoon ground cumin
¼ cup seedless raisins
2 hard-boiled eggs, coarsely chopped
12 pimiento-stuffed green olives, sliced

Sift the flour, cornmeal, baking powder, and salt into a large bowl. Cut in the lard and butter. Rub with your fingertips until the mixture resembles coarse meal. Make a well in the center and stir in the egg yolks and enough cold water (4 to 5 tablespoons) to make a soft, but not sticky, dough. This whole operation can be done in a food processor. Shape the dough into 2 balls. Wrap them in plastic wrap and refrigerate for about 30 minutes.

While the pastry chills, prepare the filling. Heat the oil in a large skillet. Add the ground beef and sauté until brown. Add the garlic, onion, potato, tomatoes (squeeze out some of the juice and seeds before adding), red pepper, and seasonings. Simmer gently for about 15 minutes. The mixture should be stiff. Remove from the heat and add the raisins, hard-boiled eggs, and olives. Set aside while you roll out the pastry.

On a lightly floured board, roll out each ball to a ⅛-inch-thick sheet. Using a cookie cutter with a 4-inch to 5-inch diameter, cut out rounds. Collect the scraps and roll out again, until all the dough is used. Keep the dough covered with a towel so that it won't dry out.

Place 1 tablespoon of the meat mixture in the center of each dough round. Lightly moisten the edges of the pastry with water. Fold each round into a half-moon shape and crimp the edges tightly. Brush the tops with the egg beaten with ½ teaspoon water. Place the empanadas on an ungreased baking sheet. Set on the middle rack of a preheated 375° F. oven for 25 to 30 minutes, until the tops turn golden brown.

These are best fresh from the oven with a chilled beer, but they can be frozen. To defrost, remove them from the freezer and place, still frozen, on a baking sheet. Let them defrost for 30 minutes. Bake them in a preheated 350° F. oven for about 15 minutes, until heated through.

Spring Rolls Welcome the New Year

Throughout China and southeast Asia, spring rolls are eaten to hail the beginning of spring, which always falls on their New Year's Day. According to tradition, spring rolls are filled with tender young bamboo shoots, the first spring onions (scallions), and crisp fresh water chestnuts—all in celebration of the year's new beginnings.

Spring rolls, whatever their country of origin, all have a wrapper (or skin) into which small bits of seasoned seafood or meat and vegetables are stuffed. The rolls are then steamed or deep-fried. You can buy either the traditional spring roll wrapper, which is round, or the square one, which is often labeled as an egg roll wrapper. Vietnamese spring rolls call for rice paper wrappers, but you need a Vietnamese grandmother to teach you how to handle these brittle skins.

Although there are subtle differences among Chinese, Thai, and Vietnamese skins, even the most finely tuned Oriental palates find it hard to tell one wrapper from the other. It is the distinctive seasonings rather than the skins that give the spring rolls their authentic character. Chinese spring rolls are usually served with hot Chinese mustard. Nam pla, the ubiquitous fish sauce distinguishes Thai spring rolls; it would be hard to find a Vietnamese spring roll that was not served with the fiery nuoc mam dipping sauce.

In the U.S., spring rolls are often called egg rolls, but this is a western corruption. It usually means that the wrapper is made with eggs. If you ask for an egg roll in China or Vietnam, no one will know what you are talking about.

Cantonese Spring Rolls

Yield: 12 spring rolls

Make more of these rolls than you think you will need. They go very fast.

If you have a choice of skins, the thinner and whiter wrappers, sometimes called "Shanghai" spring roll skins are preferable; these often can be found in Oriental specialty shops. If those are not available, the slightly thicker ones will do. You can get them either round or square. If the package says egg roll skins, it is the same thing.

The hot mustard dipping sauce should be prepared just before serving. If prepared ahead it loses some of its punch.

¼ pound fresh pork, shredded
½ pound shrimp, shelled and deveined
3 tablespoons cornstarch
½ teaspoon salt
1½ teaspoons sugar
2 teaspoons dark soy sauce
2 tablespoons oyster sauce (available in Oriental food shops)
½ teaspoon white pepper
½ cup chicken broth
2 tablespoons peanut oil
6 fresh water chestnuts, peeled and shredded
1½ cups bamboo shoots, shredded
6 to 8 scallions, cut into 1-inch pieces and shredded
1 tablespoon dry white wine
2 teaspoons sesame oil
1 egg white
12 spring roll skins
Peanut oil for deep frying
Hot Mustard Sauce

An easy way to shred the pork is to freeze it until almost solid and then place it in a food processor with the shredding disk in place. Finely dice the shrimp.

Combine the cornstarch, salt, sugar, soy sauce, oyster sauce, white pepper, and chicken broth. Set aside.

Heat a wok over high heat for 1 minute. Add the 2 tablespoons peanut oil and heat until it just begins to smoke. Add the pork to the oil, gently separating the shreds. Add the shrimp, also separating the pieces. Add the water chestnuts, bamboo shoots, and scallions and stir-fry for 1 minute. Add the white wine around the outer edge of the wok. Mix thoroughly.

Make a well in the center of the ingredients in the wok and pour in the cornstarch mixture. Combine quickly and stir-fry until the sauce becomes thick and dark. The mixture should be very stiff.

Remove from the heat, add the sesame oil, and mix well. Allow the filling to cool to room temperature. Or cover and refrigerate for a few hours or overnight.

Place a spring roll wrapper on a lightly floured flat surface. Place about 2 tablespoons of filling in a thin line about one-third of the way up the wrapper. Fold the bottom corner of the wrapper over the filling and form the filling into a log-shaped roll. Tucking in the sides as you go, roll the log up to the end of the wrapper. Seal

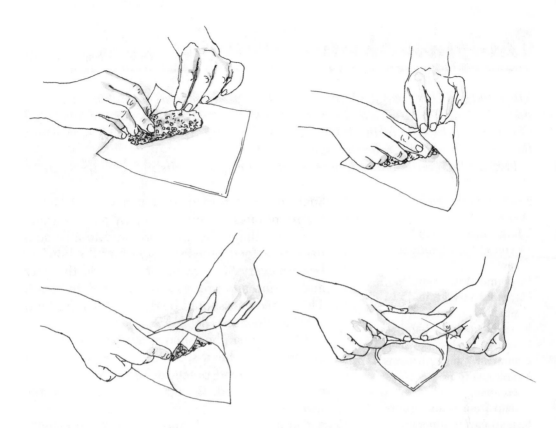

the edges by moistening them with the egg white and pressing them together gently. Repeat with the other wrappers and the remaining filling.

Heat 1½ inches of oil in a wok to 375° F. Fry the spring rolls 2 or 3 at a time until they are firm and golden brown, about 4 minutes. Drain thoroughly and serve with hot mustard.

These rolls can be frozen after cooking. To reheat, place the frozen spring rolls in a 350° F. oven and bake until hot.

Hot Mustard Sauce

½ cup dried mustard
  powder (such as
  Coleman's)
½ cup water

Combine the mustard powder and the water and mix well. If it is too thick, add a little more water. Prepared mustard won't do for this sauce; it must be the dried kind. Serve at room temperature in a small bowl.

Thai Spring Rolls

Yield: 12 spring rolls

The usual filling is meat and seafood combined with several vegetables. This version calls for bean threads and coriander root along with fish sauce (nam pla), all of which can be bought in an Oriental food market. It is the special ingredients that give these spring rolls that elusive Thai flavor.

Prepare the Garlic Sauce before making the spring rolls.

2 ounces bean threads
Warm water
2 large garlic cloves
¼ cup chopped coriander root
¼ pound raw ground pork
¼ pound raw ground shrimp
1 cup (¼ pound) bamboo shoots, fresh if possible
2 ounces fresh mushrooms
1 stalk celery
2 scallions
¾ cup fresh bean sprouts
1 small carrot, finely shredded
1 egg, slightly beaten
2 tablespoons fish sauce (nam pla)
Salt
¼ teaspoon white pepper
1 egg white
12 spring roll wrappers
Vegetable oil for frying
Garlic Dipping Sauce

Soak the bean threads in warm water to cover for 10 minutes. Drain thoroughly and set aside.

Process the garlic and coriander to a smooth paste in a food processor, scraping the bowl to be sure every bit is incorporated. Add the pork and shrimp and process a few seconds to blend. The ingredients should be thoroughly mixed but still have texture. Set aside.

Chop the bamboo shoots, mushrooms, celery, green onions, bean sprouts, and reserved bean threads in a food processor until the mixture is coarsely chopped. Do not overprocess. Add the shredded carrot.

Combine the pork and shrimp mixture with the vegetable mixture. Add the egg, fish sauce, salt to taste, and pepper. Mix thoroughly.

Place a spring roll wrapper on a lightly floured flat surface. Place about 2 tablespoons of filling one-third of the way up the wrapper. Fold the bottom edge of the wrapper over the filling and form the filling into a log-shaped roll. Tucking in the sides as you go, roll the log up to the end of the wrapper. Seal the edges by moistening them with the egg white and pressing them together gently. Repeat with the other wrappers and remaining filling.

Heat 1½ inches of oil in a wok to 375° F. Fry the spring rolls 2 or 3 at a time until they are firm and golden brown, about 4 minutes. Drain thoroughly and serve warm with the Garlic Dipping Sauce.

Garlic Dipping Sauce

½ cup water
½ cup white vinegar
½ cup sugar
1 teaspoon ground chili paste (available at Oriental specialty stores)
4 garlic cloves, finely chopped
½ teaspoon salt

Combine all the ingredients in a stainless steel or glass saucepan and boil slowly until the mixture is reduced by half. It will thicken a bit as it cools; it should have the consistency of heavy cream. If it gets too thick, add a little warm water. Serve at room temperature in a small dish.

Filipino Shrimp Lumpias

The spring roll and the lumpia have the same ancestry, although lumpias are usually a little larger and have a crêpe-like wrapper. If you don't want to make the wrappers, they are available in Oriental food markets. Prepare the Soy Dipping Sauce first and store, covered, in the refrigerator.

Filling

3 ounces shrimp, shelled, deveined, and finely chopped
¼ cup julienned bamboo shoots
2 tablespoons finely minced scallions
1 small carrot, peeled and coarsely grated
1 teaspoon soy sauce
1 garlic clove, finely minced
Salt and pepper

Wrappers

2 eggs
¼ cup cornstarch
3 tablespoons all-purpose flour
¼ teaspoon salt
½ cup water
Vegetable oil

Make the filling by combining the shrimp, bamboo shoots, scallions, carrot, soy sauce, garlic, and salt and pepper to taste in a small bowl. Refrigerate while you prepare the wrappers.

To make the wrappers, beat the eggs with a whisk in a medium-size bowl until frothy. Blend in the cornstarch, flour, and salt. Whisk in the water in a slow stream. Beat until all the ingredients are thoroughly combined.

Brush an 8-inch heavy skillet with vegetable oil and ladle 3 or 4 tablespoons of the batter into the pan, tilting quickly so that the batter covers the bottom. Return any excess batter to the bowl.

Cook over medium high heat until the wrappers are opaque and slightly blistered, about 1 minute. Turn with a spatula and cook on the other side for about 15 seconds. Slide the wrapper onto waxed paper. Repeat with the remaining batter. Wrappers can be stacked with pieces of waxed paper between each one.

Divide the filling into 4 equal portions. Place 1 portion of the filling one-fourth of the way up the wrapper. Fold the short end over the filling. Fold the left and right sides toward the center. Roll up from the bottom to form a rectangle.

Heat 1 inch of oil to 350° F. in a deep fryer or heavy skillet. Fry the lumpia, seam side down until golden brown, about 1 minute. Turn and fry on the other side for another minute. Remove with a slotted spoon or tongs and dry on paper towels.

Serve with the Soy Dipping Sauce at room temperature.

Soy Dipping Sauce

½ cup water
1 tablespoon sugar
2 tablespoons Japanese soy
 sauce
2 teaspoons cornstarch
1 garlic clove, minced
1 teaspoon minced fresh
 ginger root
Hot pepper sauce to taste

Combine all the sauce ingredients in a saucepan and cook over low heat until the sugar dissolves. Bring to a boil, stirring constantly, until the sauce thickens. Remove from heat and place in a small bowl. The sauce can be prepared several hours in advance and stored, covered, in the refrigerator.

In Search of the
Quintessential Dumpling

I consider myself somewhat of an authority on the subject of Chinese dumplings since my husband and I spent six weeks in China in search of the quintessential *chiao-tsu* (dumpling).

We were invited to China for a more serious purpose, but finding the perfect dumpling soon became, quite literally, our consuming passion. We sampled dumplings wherever we went. We stood in line early in the morning with the students at Fudan University to sample the local "grandmother's" *chiao-tsu*; we tasted the dumplings sold by vendors in the French quarter of Shanghai behind the old city; we prowled the street markets in Kunming looking for still another entry in the delicious contest we had invented.

If you want to embark on a similar quest, you do not have to wander around exotic cities, walk along beautiful beaches, visit ancient monuments, or travel to remote mountain-top villages searching for consummate dumpling. We have already done all that, and we have a winner. When we found the Jianoir-zi Restaurant in Xian, our quest was over.

Jianoir-zi is a restaurant that serves only dumplings, *chiao-tsu* of every persuasion, from tiny to baseball size, deep-fried, boiled, steamed, stuffed with food combinations that usually exist only in a gustatory fantasy.

You should go there very hungry, preferably with a Chinese friend who also loves dumplings and can read the menu, and prepare to dig in. Start with the familiar deep-fried pork wonton and the half-moon fish dumplings with the scalloped edge, and then move on to the steamed shrimp dumplings in a wrapper molded like the old-fashioned cap once worn by Dutch children.

If you come early you can find *siu mai*, the-cook-and-sell dumpling. These dumplings are so named because they are shaped like small cooking kettles filled with irresistible morsels and are so beautiful that they are sure to sell first.

There are the familiar pot-stickers. You can sample the Phoenix-eyes dumplings shaped to look like a woman's eyes, and then feast on the perfectly symmetrical dumplings that resemble a pagoda. Some are served in the bamboo multilayered steamers in which they were cooked. The deep-fried dumplings come to the table still sizzling.

A proper dumpling meal can take two hours. Never mind that you've lingered so long eating dumplings that you almost miss the bus to the Museum of the Qin Pottery Figures, which you traveled 10,000 miles to visit. The 6,000 full-sized terra cotta soldiers in their burial ground will be there for another 5000 years but the dumpling chef won't.

In a Chinese home, making dumplings is a family endeavor. Usually preparing the skins is entrusted to the oldest woman in the family, but stuffing the dumplings is done by all who eat. Since Chinese kitchens are the size of a closet, the stuffers gather at the dining room table to work and chat. This custom hasn't changed in hundreds of years.

I was given private lessons on how to stuff dumplings in the home of a Chinese friend. The hard work — making the skins and preparing the filling — had already been done in the kitchen. I just had to put the filling in the skins and seal them properly. Like a Chinese puzzle, shaping dumplings is a lot more difficult than it looks.

My teachers (5 of them) were very patient, showing me exactly where to place my American fingers, and although I thought I was doing it just right, my dumplings never looked like theirs. I am sure that the ones that fell apart in the boiling water were the ones I had formed, although my host was polite enough to blame it on his clumsy son-in-law. I was glad that I was not being judged as a prospective bride. More than once I heard that in old China, a bridegroom's mother could reject a prospective daughter-in-law if she could not make a proper dumpling.

Deep-Fried Wontons

Yield: About 50 wontons

In Chinese homes they often make one large batch of dumplings. For variety, some are deep-fried and the rest are boiled. They taste very different.

2 tablespoons peanut oil
½ pound lean ground pork
1 pound raw shrimp, peeled and deveined, washed, and thoroughly dried
2 tablespoons soy sauce
1 tablespoon Chinese rice wine
1 teaspoon salt
6 fresh water chestnuts, peeled, washed, dried, and finely chopped (or use canned)
1 large scallion, including some of the green top, finely chopped
1 teaspoon cornstarch dissolved in 1 tablespoon cold water
50 square wonton wrappers (available at Oriental specialty stores)
3 cups peanut oil

Place a 12-inch wok or a 10-inch heavy skillet over high heat until it is very hot, about 30 seconds. Pour in 2 tablespoons of oil and heat for another 30 seconds. The oil should not smoke. Add the pork and stir-fry for about 1 minute, until the meat loses its reddish color. Add the shrimp, soy sauce, wine, salt, water chestnuts, and scallions and stir-fry for another minute. Add the cornstarch mixture and stir constantly until the liquid thickens. Transfer the contents to a bowl and cool to room temperature.

Spread out the wonton wrappers on a flat surface. The wrappers not being used should be kept covered with a dish towel. Place 1½ teaspoons of the filling in a cylinder shape in the center of each wrapper. Fold the corner of the wrapper over the filling at an angle to make two askew triangles. Gently pull down the bottom corners of the triangle around the base and overlap the tips of the corners. Wet your finger and pinch the tips. The filling should be completely enclosed.

As the wontons are finished, place them on a lightly floured flat plate and cover them with dry towel. If they cannot be fried within 30 minutes, cover them with a plastic wrap and refrigerate them.

Set a 12-inch wok over high heat and add the 3 cups of oil. Heat to 375° F. and deep-fry the wontons, about 10 at a time, for about 2 minutes, until they are crisp and golden. Drain on paper towels. Serve on a heated platter.

These wontons should be served very hot. They can be kept warm in a 250° F. oven for up to an hour.

78

Street Food

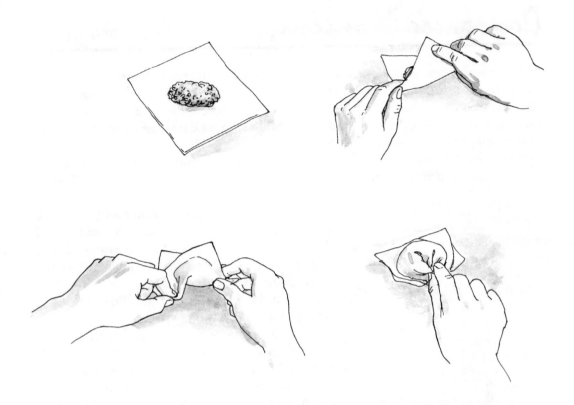

Cantonese Dumplings

Yield: 70 dumplings

These steamed dumplings are a favorite of Chinese children who greet them with the same enthusiasm American children show for hamburgers. To be authentic, the dumpling skin should be made with wheat starch, which can be bought in a Chinese specialty shop. Supermarket wonton skins work well and are much more convenient, but the taste is a little different.

If you want to steam dumplings at home, a Chinese steamer is a good investment. Bamboo steamers are traditional, but aluminum ones are also available.

2½ tablespoons fresh pork fat trimmed from pork chops or fresh ham
¾ pound shrimp, shelled and deveined, washed, thoroughly dried, and finely diced
1 teaspoon salt
1½ teaspoons sugar
1 small egg white, beaten
1½ tablespoons tapioca flour
2 teaspoons oyster sauce (available in Oriental food stores)
1 teaspoon sesame oil
White pepper
⅓ cup diced water chestnuts
⅓ cup finely chopped scallions (white portion only)
¼ cup diced bamboo shoots
70 three-inch round wonton skins (*shao mai*)

Place the pork fat in boiling water and boil until it is translucent. Remove from the water and place the pork in a bowl of cold water. Let it stand for a few minutes, then remove it. Dry the fat thoroughly and finely dice.

Using a food processor, combine the diced shrimp with the salt, sugar, egg white, tapioca flour, oyster sauce, sesame oil, and white pepper to taste. Mix thoroughly, using a few on/off turns and scraping the bowl once or twice. Add the cooked pork fat, water chestnuts, scallions, and bamboo shoots. Combine evenly and thoroughly with a few more on/off turns. An electric beater can also be used, but process a little longer.

Place the mixture in a shallow dish, cover, and refrigerate for about 4 hours, or place in the freezer for 30 minutes.

To fill the dumplings, loosely cup a wrapper in the palm of your hand. Place a tablespoon of the filling in the cup. With your other hand, gather up the sides of the wrapper, pleating it all the way up. The dough should hug the filling up the sides but the filling should *not* be enclosed at the top. Gently squeeze the middle of the cup to give it a wasp-waist shape. Tap the bottom of the dumpling on the table to flatten the bottom so that it can stand upright.

The dumplings can be made ahead, placed on a lightly floured plate, and refrigerated for several hours (no more) before steaming.

Steam for 7 to 10 minutes in a Chinese steamer or on a rack of a regular steamer and serve immediately.

If the dumplings are done in several batches, keep the finished ones warm by covering them with a lid of a large saucepan.

Indian Snacks: Samosas, Pakoras, Bhelpuris

Most Indians are vegetarians. Since they do not eat meat, they get their protein from dried peas and beans. This might seem like uninteresting fare, but add some vegetables, and season with hot chiles, turmeric, garlic, and grated coconut and meat seems less important.

As you wander through an Indian bazaar you quickly get the idea that Indians are dedicated to non-stop snacking. Pretzel-like pastries called *murukkus*, potato crisps with red hot chiles, crisp rice cakes with cashews and peanuts seem to be on every corner. Along the beaches, gaily striped wooden stalls offer countless variations of *bhelpuri*, one of India's favorite snacks. The basic ingredients of *bhelpuri* are puffed rice, lentils, toasted peanuts, herbs, and chutney, but the combinations are endless.

Pakoras, a savory vegetable fritter, are another favorite snack food. They can be made using whatever vegetable is at hand—bits of cauliflower, eggplant, potatoes, green chiles, spinach leaves—dipped in a batter of chickpea flour and deep-fried. Samosas, which are often sold at the same stalls as pakoras, are triangular cakes that can be filled with highly seasoned vegetables or meat. When the aromas of frying pakoras and samosas coalesce they create a spicy fragrance that perfumes the air.

If you crave a real samosa adventure, all you have to do is travel to Pilani in Rajasthan state. There is a spot right behind the post office on the campus of the Birla Institute where a samosa vendor has been making the quintessential samosas for many years; his fame is legendary throughout the area. But, his output is limited; he makes about two hundred samosas only three times a day: at eight in the morning, noon, and midnight. Why these odd hours? Well, it seems that he has another job and these are the only times he can get away.

People are willing to wait for hours to enjoy his samosas, but unfortunately, so are the kites. Kites are swift, hawk-like birds that combine the keenest vision with a unique ability to zero in on a small object. They fly so high above that they are almost impossible to spot with the naked eye, and they remain out of sight until the moment that the samosas appear. Then they drop from the sky like a stone, their large wings tucked close to their bodies, pluck a samosa from the hand of an unlucky victim, and rise up to the heavens to enjoy their stolen pleasure. It seems that these thieves never miss, never peck a hand with their sharp beaks, nor touch anyone with their wings.

Spicy Potato Samosas

Yield: 30 samosas

The original samosas were fried dumplings made of peas and potatoes. But like many street foods, they have become more elaborate over the years. You can get samosas filled with ground lamb, nuts, and raisins and served with a dipping sauce.

Pastry

3 cups all-purpose flour
½ teaspoon salt
3 tablespoons ghee or
   clarified butter (see
   page 55)
¾ cup ice water

Spicy Potato Filling

2 tablespoons vegetable oil
1 medium-size onion, finely
   chopped
1 (10-ounce) package frozen
   peas, defrosted and
   drained
1 tablespoon finely grated,
   peeled fresh ginger root
1 fresh hot green chile
   pepper, finely chopped
3 tablespoons finely chopped
   cilantro (fresh coriander
   or Chinese parsley)
3 tablespoons water
1½ pounds new potatoes,
   boiled in their jackets,
   peeled, and cut into
   ¼-inch dices
1½ teaspoons salt
1 teaspoon ground coriander
1 teaspoon garam masala
1 teaspoon ground cumin
¼ teaspoon cayenne pepper
2 tablespoons lemon juice
2 cups vegetable oil

Sift the flour with the salt into a deep bowl. Add the ghee and combine with your fingertips until the mixture resembles coarse meal. Pour the water over the mixture all at once, knead vigorously, and form the dough into a ball. If it crumbles, add up to 4 more tablespoons of water, one at a time, until the particles adhere. On a lightly floured surface, knead the dough by folding it and pressing it down and pushing it backward for about 10 minutes, until it is smooth.

Making the dough can also be done in a food processor. Place the flour and salt in the work bowl. Add the ghee and process with 10 to 12 on/off turns. Pour in the ice water and process until the mixture becomes a dough. Add a little more water, if needed. No vigorous kneading is necessary.

Form the dough into a ball, brush it lightly with ghee or oil, and place it in a bowl. Cover with a damp towel to keep it moist. Let it rest for at least 30 minutes. The dough can remain at room temperature for up to 5 hours.

While the dough rests, prepare the filling. Heat 2 tablespoons oil in large skillet. Add the onion and stir-fry over medium heat for a few minutes, until the onion is lightly brown. Add the peas, ginger, green chile, cilantro, and water. Cover and simmer until the peas are cooked, stirring occasionally and adding a little more water, if necessary.

Add the diced potatoes, salt, ground coriander, garam masala, cumin, cayenne, and lemon juice. Turn off the heat and allow the mixture to cool. Cover and refrigerate for 30 minutes.

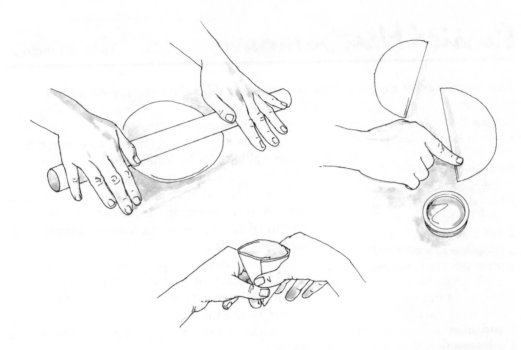

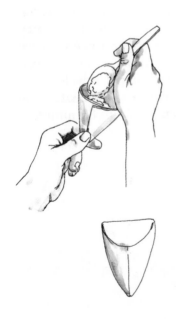

To shape the samosas, divide the dough into fourths. On a lightly floured board, roll out one piece of dough as thinly as possible (very important). Keep the unused dough covered. With a large cookie cutter or a glass, cut out about fifteen 6-inch circles. Cut each circle in half.

Moisten the edges of the dough with your finger dipped in water. Holding the semicircle of dough in your hand, shape it into a cone. Fill the cone with 1 tablespoon of the filling. Moisten and press the top edge over the filling to form a tight triangle. Repeat with the remaining dough and filling. The pastries may be kept on a lightly floured plate, covered, for 2 to 3 hours before they are fried.

To fry the samosas, heat the 2 cups vegetable oil in a deep heavy skillet or in a deep fryer to 375° F. Deep-fry the turnovers, a few at a time, for 2 to 3 minutes, turning once, until they turn golden brown. Drain on paper towels. Serve hot. They can be kept warm in a 200° F. oven in a baking dish lined with paper towels.

These samosas can be frozen. To reheat, place frozen in a 400° F. oven for 25 to 30 minutes.

Curried Meat Samosas

This recipe makes delicious samosas, much milder than the previous ones.

Samosa Pastry (page 84)
1 pound lean ground lamb
3 tablespoons oil
1 medium-size onion, finely
  chopped
1 tart green apple, cored
  and finely chopped
1 garlic clove, minced
2 teaspoons ground cumin
2 teaspoons finely minced
  fresh ginger root
1 teaspoon turmeric
½ teaspoon ground
  coriander
1½ teaspoons salt
¼ teaspoon black pepper
¼ teaspoon crushed dried
  red peppers
2 tablespoons fruit chutney
¼ cup dark raisins
⅓ cup coarsely chopped raw
  cashew nuts
3 to 4 tablespoons yogurt

Prepare the pastry as directed.

To make the filling, brown the meat in a heavy skillet over high heat until it loses its reddish color. Drain thoroughly and set aside.

In a large skillet, heat the oil over moderate heat. Add the onion, apple, and garlic and sauté just until tender. Add the cumin, ginger root, turmeric, coriander, salt, black pepper, and red pepper and sauté, stirring, for 5 minutes.

Add the browned meat, chutney, raisins, and cashews. Remove from the heat and add enough yogurt so the mixture just holds together but is not mushy. Chill in the refrigerator for several hours.

Roll out the pastry dough and fill as directed.

To fry the samosas, heat the 2 cups vegetable oil in a deep heavy skillet or in a deep fryer to 375° F. Deep-fry the turnovers, a few at a time, for 2 to 3 minutes, turning once, until they turn golden brown. Drain on paper towels. Serve hot. They can be kept warm in a 200° F. oven in a baking dish lined with paper towels.

These samosas can be frozen. To reheat, place frozen in a 400° F. oven for 25 to 30 minutes.

English Pies Go Back to Simple Simon

English savory pies go way back to Shakespeare's time and even before. Simple Simon could have met a pieman going to the fair in the early 1700s. We know that meat and fish pies were sold on the streets of London as late as the nineteenth century, until the opening of proper pie-shops.

Of course, the street vendors did not accept the encroachment of the pie shops without a fight. As vendors saw their livelihood being eroded by these fancy new shops, some inventive lads started a game called "tossing the pieman." A coin would be tossed but never by the pieman. The pieman would call out heads or tails. If he won, he would be paid without giving up the pie; if he lost the pie was free.

Since the game was more related to gambling than to hunger, many more pies were "won" than eaten. The uneaten pies wound up being tossed at the crowd or at the pieman, if he didn't disappear fast enough. Variations of this game can be found in distant places to this day. On the beaches of Alexandria in Egypt, you can toss the vendor for a sesame bread. They say that it tastes better that way.

Perhaps the most famous English savory is the Cornish pastie (rhymes with vastly), started in Cornwall, England, as dinner for the miners. The men who worked in the mines had to have a nourishing meal in the middle of the day and the pastie served that purpose. Many logistical burdens were placed on this meal. Not only did it have to nourish the miners, it had to survive the morning, a major feat in itself. A mine is no place for a delicate man or a delicate meal. In fact, the dough of the pastie had to be firm enough to withstand being dropped down the mine shaft.

Mine dining presented a unique set of etiquette dilemmas. For one thing, washing-up facilities were nonexistent and coal dust was everywhere. Some wives fashioned a disposable half-moon handle made of solid dough at one end of the pastie to accommodate the miner's blackened thumb. He was then able to eat without incorporating all the dust on his hands into his food. After he finished his dinner, he threw the handle away.

The wives would mark the pasties on one end with the initials of the person for whom it was intended. If he followed the rules, the husband would begin eating the pastie from the unmarked end so he could find it again later, if he wanted to save some for a snack. Marking one's initials on a Cornish pastie has become a tradition.

Cornish Pasties

There are several variations on the pastie crust. You can use your favorite short crust or flaky pastry or try a traditional hot water crust.

The filling does not vary much. The steak must be of excellent quality or it will be tough. All the ingredients for the filling must be raw. Nothing is sautéed before placing it in the crust. The filling should be highly seasoned with white pepper.

Try substituting leeks for onions, or lamb for the beef. It changes the flavor, but the idea is the same.

Hot Water Crust

4 cups all-purpose flour
1 teaspoon salt
½ cup water
1 cup butter and/or lard

Filling

4 medium-size potatoes, peeled
1 medium-size onion, finely diced
1 medium-size turnip, peeled and diced
¾ pound chuck steak, finely diced
¼ cup roughly chopped fresh parsley
2 tablespoons butter
Salt and white pepper
1 egg, beaten

Sift together the flour and salt. In a large pan, combine the water with the butter and bring to a boil. Beat in the flour and salt and cook, stirring constantly, until the dough pulls away from the pan and looks transparent.

Place the dough on a well-floured board and knead into a ball. Cut the dough into quarters, and roll each quarter into a circle ¼-inch thick. Work quickly; the pastry will crack if allowed to cool.

Cut the potatoes by "shripping" them, that is cutting them into very fine slices as you constantly turn the potato in your hand. Put a few pieces of potato in the center of each pastry round. Add some diced onion and diced turnip and some diced meat. Add some chopped parsley and dot with butter. Season well with salt and pepper to taste, and add a few more potato slices to keep the filling moist.

Using a brush, dampen the edges of the pastry with water and pull half the dough over to meet the other half, forming a half circle. Pinch the edges with your fingers to make a tight seal. If you can make the edge into a wavy line (it takes some practice), you have an authentic Cornish crimp. Using a toothpick or a pin, prick the appropriate initials in the corner of each pastie. Brush the pastry with the egg and set on a greased cookie sheet. Repeat with the remaining pastry.

Bake in a preheated 425° F. oven for 10 minutes. Reduce the oven temperature to 350° F.

and continue baking another 30 to 40 minutes, until golden. Serve hot or cold. They will keep warm if wrapped in a tea towel.

These pasties freeze well and make superb picnic fare. They should be brought to room temperature before reheating for 10 minutes at 250° F. They can also be eaten at room temperature, as they usually are in England.

Note: If you do not initial the tops of the pasties, make a little hole in the middle of the crust to let the steam escape.

Piroshkis: A Slavic Savory

Piroshkis are delicious meat pies that trace their origins back to Slavic peasant fare. In Eastern Europe they are as popular as pasta is in Italy and come in about as many forms. They range in size from walnut to apple and vary in texture from the lightest soufflé to dense and chewy.

Throughout Eastern Europe it is common to see jumbo-sized women standing over vats of bubbling oil, deep-frying these dumplings for an on-the-spot snack; they are usually wrapped in a newspaper cone. It's a good idea to wait a minute or two and let the paper absorb some of the fat in which the piroskis have been swimming. They are not on anyone's reducing diet.

As with so many ethnic foods, it is possible to sample piroshkis (some-times called pirogies) throughout Eastern Europe and never eat the same one twice. Fillings can consist of mixtures of meat, fish, eggs, cabbage, cheese, kasha, or potatoes, and that's just for starters. Alone or in combination, there are literally hundreds of different fillings for these wonderful meat pies.

In large cities throughout the U.S., street fairs seem to beckon vendors who grew up with these delicacies in their homes and haven't forgotten what their grandmothers taught them. Piroshkis, with their glorious fillings, are prepared ahead at home, and then, as in the old country, boiled or fried on the street. A serving is usually 2 or 3, with or without sour cream.

Beef-Filled Piroshkis

Yield: 48 piroshkis

The piroshkis sold by street vendors are likely to be deep-fried rather than baked so that they do not have to be cooked in advance. Baked piroshkis are usually made at home.

The pastry used in this recipe is easier to handle than the lard and butter pastry which is more authentic. It is a delicious adaptation.

Pastry

1 pound cream cheese, at
    room temperature
1 pound unsalted butter, at
    room temperature
4 cups sifted all-purpose
    flour
1 teaspoon salt

Filling

¼ cup butter
3 cups finely chopped onions
2 pounds extra-lean ground
    beef
4 hard-boiled eggs, finely
    chopped
6 tablespoons finely snipped
    fresh dill or 2 teaspoons
    dried
2 teaspoons salt
½ teaspoon black pepper

To make the pastry, combine the cream cheese and 1 pound butter and mix until they are well blended. Add the flour and salt and mix thoroughly. This can be done in a food processor. Form into 2 balls, wrap in plastic wrap, and refrigerate for at least 2 hours.

In a large heavy skillet, melt the ¼ cup butter. Add the onions and cook over high heat until they are soft and transparent but not brown, stirring occasionally. Add the meat and mash with a fork to break up any lumps. Cook until the meat loses its pink color. Place the onion-meat mixture in a food processor and process until smooth. Combine the mixture with the eggs, dill, salt, and pepper. Mix thoroughly and adjust the seasoning. Cool and place in the refrigerator while rolling out the dough.

Remove 1 ball of the chilled dough from the refrigerator. Pinch off chunks of dough about 1¼ inches in size and roll each quickly into a ball. Place each ball between 2 sheets of waxed paper and roll it out to a circle about 3 inches in diameter.

Drop 1½ tablespoons of filling in the center of each circle of dough and flatten it slightly. The mixture should be dry. Moisten the edges of the dough with water. Fold the dough over to make a closed semicircle. Press the edges of pastry together with the tines of a fork; be sure to seal well. Repeat with the other balls of dough.

Place the filled piroshkis on an ungreased baking sheet and bake in a preheated 375° F. oven for 15 to 20 minutes, until they are golden brown. Let them stand for a few minutes before serving.

Knishes: The Ultimate Nosh

The knish that started in Jewish homes as an holiday accompaniment to meat has become a savory delicacy as a street food. It is best not to discuss how to make knishes with a person who professes to be a "knish maven." It finally gets down to whose grandmother was a better cook. You can't win; the best you can hope for is a culinary stand-off.

In a streamlined form, the knish has joined the cocktail party circuit, as a tidbit that goes with drinks. Eat enough knishes and who cares if dinner ever comes.

When I was a child, the knish was part of my Saturday ritual. Everyone I knew went to a movie matinee on Saturday afternoon, preceded by lunch at the local delicatessen. Lunch never varied: a hot dog with mustard and sauerkraut and a sizzling knish. These were washed down with a cream soda or a celery tonic. If this combination ever resulted in indigestion, I don't recall the pain. Considering that these knishes were of the mass-produced variety and probably had been sitting on the steam table for days, I can't believe they were really as delicious as I remember them. But, my childhood recollection persists. I still find the knish (and the hot dog) hard to resist.

Cheese-Filled Knishes

Yield: 24 knishes

Knish Dough (page 92)
3 tablespoons butter
1½ cups diced scallions
   (onions can be substituted)
3 cups dry cottage cheese or
   farmer's cheese
2 eggs
3 tablespoons sour cream
2 tablespoons sugar
1½ teaspoons salt
½ teaspoon white pepper

Prepare the dough as directed.

Melt the butter in a skillet. Add the scallions and sauté until limp. Cool to room temperature. Blend in all the other ingredients. The mixture should be stiff. Fill the pastry and bake as directed on page 92.

Potato Knishes

Dough

2 cups sifted all-purpose
  flour
1 teaspoon baking powder
½ teaspoon salt
2 tablespoons water
1 tablespoon vegetable oil
2 eggs, well beaten

Filling

6 tablespoons chicken fat or
  butter
1 cup chopped onions
2 cups well-mashed potatoes
1 egg
1 teaspoon salt
½ teaspoon white pepper

To make the dough, sift together the flour, baking powder, and salt onto a board. Make a well in the center and add the water, oil, and eggs. Using your hand, mix well and knead until a smooth dough forms. Let the dough rest for a few minutes.

Meanwhile, make the filling. Melt the chicken fat in a frying pan. Add the onions and sauté until browned, about 5 minutes. Combine with all the other ingredients. Beat until fluffy; there should be no lumps. Set aside.

Divide the dough in half and, working one piece at a time on a lightly floured board, roll out the dough as thin as possible (⅛ inch). Keep the dough you are not using covered with a dish towel; it dries out easily.

Use a 3-inch glass or cookie cutter to form about 24 circles of dough. Place a tablespoon of filling on each circle. Moisten the edges of the pastry with water. Draw the edges together to form a semicircle, pinch firmly to form a tight seal. To make a larger, round (and perhaps slightly more authentically shaped) knish, place a scant 2 tablespoons of filling on each circle and top with a second circle of dough.

Place on a lightly oiled baking sheet and bake in a preheated 375° F. oven for 35 minutes, or until browned. Serve hot.

Potato Dough Knishes

Yield: About 20 knishes

Some feel that the only authentic knish is the potato knish. Even if you agree that this is so, be prepared to argue about the authentic size. This recipe for 2-inch knishes may not suit the big-knish contingent.

These knishes make a superb side dish for a holiday meal.

5 tablespoons chicken fat or butter
¾ cup chopped onion
4 cups thoroughly mashed potatoes
¾ cup potato flour (can be found in the Jewish specialty section of a supermarket)
3 eggs
1½ teaspoons salt
½ teaspoon white pepper

Melt 3 tablespoons of the chicken fat in a skillet. Add the onions and cook slowly until they are quite brown but not burned. The longer the onions cook, the sweeter they will be. If you prefer a stronger onion taste, cook only until limp. Cool and set aside. The onions can be covered and refrigerated overnight.

Melt the remaining 2 tablespoons chicken fat and combine with the remaining ingredients. Mix (with your hand) until the mixture is smooth; there should be no lumps of potato. This mixture can be covered and refrigerated overnight.

With floured hands, break off pieces of dough and flatten them into 2-inches circles. You can use a 2-inch glass for this purpose. Place about ¾ teaspoon of the browned onions (or less) on each piece of dough and top with another round of dough. Pinch the edges together tightly to enclose the filling. Place on a greased baking sheet.

Bake in a preheated 375° F. oven for about 20 minutes, or until brown. Serve hot.

The Perfect Potato

Baking a potato provides instant success. Never mind that it is one of the few foods that cannot be ruined no matter how dim the cook. If you remembered to heat the oven to approximately the correct temperature, nothing can go wrong. Could all cooking be this easy?

A baked potato with butter and salt does more than just satisfy hunger; it passes all the tests of a true comfort food. A baked potato takes us back to childhood pleasures. It was often the first food offered after an illness. "You can have a baked potato today," meant that healthy days were ahead.

Peruvian Indians grew potatoes 3000 years ago. Potatoes traveled to Europe in the sixteenth century as food fit only for livestock and the poorest people. Then they made the return trip to the New World carried by Irish settlers. By then, the potato was also known as the Murphy.

In the 1800s baked potatoes were sold by street vendors in London from a tin pan mounted on 4 legs, called a potato can. It was an elaborate self-contained contraption that could be worn around the vendor's neck (if he had a strong neck). It used charcoal to roast the potatoes and then kept them hot over boiling water. At one end of the can was a small pipe for carrying off steam. At the other end was a small compartment for butter and salt. As the vendor prospered, the potato can turned into a gilded cart, often with brass fittings.

The only taste that rivals a plain baked potato is a stuffed potato. Today's potato vendors can be found from the streets of Lima to the streets of London. There are at least 40 documented potato stuffings; in fact, almost anything you fancy can be stuffed into a warmed baked potato. Grated cheddar cheese with or without fried onions and chopped pickle, bits of crisp bacon, chopped prawns, ground meats, curried chicken, even baked beans are for the moderately adventurous eaters. If you want something really unusual, travel to Scotland, and try baked potatoes stuffed with haggis.

Walk around the streets of London today and you can see potato carts just like the ones used in Victorian times at Covent Garden. They still have red handles and yellow wheels trimmed with brass, and a medallion that proclaims that they have been properly registered. You can still see the same 3 brass drawers that store the hot potatoes as they did in the days of Queen Victoria. The handles even have the old spanner box for tools needed to mend the cart or repair a wheel.

I asked one vendor if they were true Victorian carts. "No, just clever imitations." He immediately offered me a card that explained how to rent such a cart for my next special festive occasion. I would have preferred to think that I had stepped back into the last century. Sorry I asked!

Stuffed Baked Potatoes

Yield: 8 stuffed potatoes

4 large baking potatoes,
  baked
2 tablespoons melted butter
8 ounces cheddar cheese,
  shredded
6 bacon slices, fried until
  crisp, crumbled
3 scallions, finely chopped
Sour cream and chives
  (optional)

Cut the potatoes in half lengthwise. Scoop out carefully, leaving ¼ inch of the potato in the skin.

Mash about 1 cup of the pulp and combine with the melted butter, cheese, bacon, and scallions. It should be a fairly smooth mixture. Add a little more potato pulp, if necessary.

Pack the mixture into the potato skins and mound slightly. Arrange the potatoes in a baking pan and bake at 325° F. until the cheese is thoroughly melted, about 15 minutes. Serve immediately with sour cream and chives.

Pizza: An International Love Affair

Pizza, like so many good things (printing, clocks, the magnetic compass) is said to have started in China. Food historians cite thirteenth-century writings to prove that when Marco Polo returned to Venice from Cambuloc (now Beijing), he brought back samples of foods that he enjoyed in the Orient. One was a large flat loaf topped with slices of meat and cheese called *peenzah*.

A challenge to Marco Polo comes from the Greeks who claim that *they* introduced pizza to the world. If one asks for proof that the Greeks are the true source of this world-famous concoction, they point out that a pizza-like dish was mentioned in Plato's *Republic*.

During the time they occupied the southernmost regions of Italy, circa 730 B.C., the Greeks baked a flat bread that they called *plakuntos*. This served as an edible plate for an assortment of local bounty: olive oil, garlic, herbs, vegetables, and cheese. When it was adopted by the Romans, *plakuntos* became *placenta*, a pie made of the finest flours, topped with cheese mixed with honey and seasoned with bay leaves and oil. It was baked on the floor of the hearth, right next to the burning wood. The word pizza comes from the corruption of the Latin *picea*, the word used for the dark coating under the placenta, which was a result of the burning ash.

Who really invented pizza? I guess it comes down to a question of faith or historical preference. Whom do you believe, Plato or Marco Polo? No matter who is responsible for the introduction of the pizza to the western world, the Neapolitans claim that Naples is its spiritual home. It was there that tomatoes were added, and it is tomatoes that give pizza its true character.

Pizza was brought to the United States in the poor immigrant's meager baggage. It literally sustained life for impoverished Neapolitans as they made their way in the New World. In poor Italian neighborhoods in New York, no immigrant could even dream of the luxury of store-bought bread. Italian women prepared their own dough at home and paid the local baker a penny to bake the bread in his oven in the afternoon when the oven wasn't being used.

The hour coincided with the time when the children were returning from school, ravenous as all children are at that hour. Their mothers would put into the oven a few extra pieces of flat dough flavored with garlic, tomato sauce, oregano, and coarse salt. These smaller pieces were always ready before the bread was baked and were offered for immediate consumption to stave off starvation. These scraps were called *focaccia*, just as they were in the old country. No banquet could have tasted better to a child (or adult) than that fragrant chewy bread, hot from the oven, warming the hands as well as the stomach.

The first pizzeria was started in

New York's Little Italy in 1905, but it didn't stir much interest, even in the Italian community. It ambled along in second gear until after World War II, when some nameless *pizzaiolo* (pizza-maker) employed his good-for-nothing son-in-law, a would-be juggler, to shape the pizza dough and to put it in the oven, which just happened to be in the front window. To relieve the tedium of the job, the juggler began doing what he knew best—tossing the balls of dough, one at a time, two at a time, catching one on his elbow, the other on his index finger. Crowds gathered to watch the show and, of course, eat the pizza.

There, in that small shop with its juggling oven-boy, began a world-wide love affair. It is safe to say that the popularity of pizza throughout the world is rivaled only by the popularity of blue jeans. At this very moment in downtown Beijing, pizzas are being scarfed down by Chinese who may be unaware that they are completing the doughy circle that Marco Polo began so many years ago.

Pizza Margherita

This is a variation of the classic Neapolitan pizza, named for the pizza-loving Queen Margherita of Italy. The red tomatoes, the white mozzarella, and the bright green basil honor the Italian flag.

If this pizza seems bland, additional toppings, such as sliced pepperoni, mushrooms, anchovies, sausage, and so on, can be added during the last 5 minutes of baking. The pizza will be more zesty, but it will no longer be an authentic Pizza Margherita.

Pizza Dough

2 packages (2 tablespoons)
   active dry yeast
1 cup lukewarm water
   (105° F.)
3½ cups all-purpose flour
1½ teaspoons salt
3 tablespoons olive oil

Pizza Topping

3 pounds vine-ripened plum
   tomatoes or 3 (1-pound)
   cans Italian tomatoes
3 tablespoons olive oil
½ teaspoon salt
3 tablespoons finely chopped
   fresh basil leaves, or 2
   teaspoons dried, finely
   crumbled
2 cups shredded mozzarella
   cheese (about 1 pound)

Dissolve the yeast in the water and let it stand for 10 minutes. Combine the flour and the salt in a large mixing bowl. Make a well in the center and pour in the oil and the yeast mixture. Beat the flour into the liquid and gather the dough into a ball. Turn the dough onto a well-floured board, and knead for 12 to 15 minutes. Punch it down with the heel of your hand, push it away, and fold it over. Slap the dough on a hard surface occasionally. Add more flour as needed to keep it from sticking. When the dough is light and elastic, and no longer sticky, form it into a smooth ball.

Place the dough in a lightly oiled bowl, cover, and set the bowl in a warm place (on the top of the refrigerator) to rise for an hour, or until doubled in volume.

Meanwhile, prepare the topping. If you are using fresh tomatoes cover them, a few at a time, with boiling water and slip off the skins. Squeeze out the seeds and the juice and cut them into large chunks. If you are using canned tomatoes, drain them thoroughly in a colander and coarsely chop them.

In a small bowl, combine the tomatoes, oil, salt, and basil. Set aside.

Punch the dough down and knead it a few times. Shape it into a ball and let it rise again for an hour. The dough is now ready to use.

Note: After the first rising, the dough can be punched down and refrigerated or frozen. If frozen, thaw in the refrigerator overnight. Let the dough come to room temperature (about 2 hours) before letting it rise for the second time.

When you are ready to assemble the pizza, place the oven rack in the lowest position and preheat the oven to 425° F. Prepare the pizza pans by lightly greasing them and dusting with cornmeal.

Divide the dough in half. On a lightly floured board, roll out each half about ¼ inch thick. With each half, form one 14-inch round or two 7-inch rounds. If you like a little thicker crust, make the rounds smaller. Turn up the edges of crust slightly. If there is any delay in using the dough, cover it with a cloth to keep it from drying out.

With oiled fingers stretch the dough onto the pan, pushing for a ½-inch rim all around. Spoon on the tomato-oil mixture, going up to the rim. Place in the preheated oven and bake for 20 minutes. Remove the pizza from the oven and add the grated mozzarella and sprinkle with a few drops of olive oil (this prevents the cheese from drying out). Return to the oven and bake for 5 more minutes until the rim gets crusty and brown. Repeat shaping and filling with the other piece of the dough while the first pizza is in the oven.

Remove the pizza from the oven and allow it to stand for 5 minutes before serving. It's easier on the roof of the mouth.

Pissaladière

No serious French cook would even permit the notion that anything edible could come from the Italian side of the Alps. So, when pizza migrated to France, it received refinement and a new name: Pizza of Naples became pissaladière of Nice.

The bread dough became a buttery pie-shaped pastry shell. Pepperoni disappeared; it was much too rough for sensitive French palates. Instead the pastry was filled with the bounty of the south of France: sautéed onions, black olives, and anchovy fillets. A debate over the proper use of tomato sauce raged. To appease both factions, pissaladière was often served with one half covered with tomato sauce and the other half without any.

A thick layer of onions is essential for a good pissaladière; it should be at least half as thick as the crust. If a short crust is used, the onion layer should be of the same thickness as the crust. This pissaladière has no tomatoes. If you prefer it with tomatoes, peel, seed, and coarsely chop 1½ pounds ripe tomatoes and add it to the filling just before the cheese. Do not use canned olives. It will look as good but it will taste different.

Pissaladière can be served as snack or an appetizer.

Filling

½ cup olive oil
2 pounds yellow onions, sliced very thin
1 teaspoon sugar
1 garlic clove, finely minced
½ teaspoon salt
1 tablespoon fresh thyme leaves or ½ teaspoon dried
1 tablespoon fresh oregano leaves or ½ teaspoon dried
½ cup shredded Gruyère cheese
6 anchovies, minced
½ cup black olives (Niçoise), pitted and cut in slivers

First, make the filling. In a large heavy skillet, heat 6 tablespoons of the oil over medium heat. Add the onions and cook until softened, about 5 minutes, stirring occasionally. Add the sugar and the garlic to the onions, and cook until the onions are golden, about 20 minutes.

In a small bowl, combine the remaining 2 tablespoons of the oil with the salt, thyme, and oregano. Set aside.

Drain the onions into a colander which has been placed over a bowl and reserve the oil in the bowl to add to the crust.

Crust

2 packages (2 tablespoons)
  active dry yeast
½ teaspoon sugar
¼ cup lukewarm water
2 to 3 cups all-purpose flour
½ teaspoon salt
1 garlic clove, minced
½ teaspoon crumbled dried
  rosemary (optional)
2 eggs, lightly beaten

To make the crust, combine the yeast and sugar in a small bowl. Add the water. Stir it once and let it stand until the yeast has dissolved and the mixture is bubbly.

Measure 1 cup of the flour into a large mixing bowl and add the salt, garlic, and rosemary. Stir in the yeast mixture. Add 2 tablespoons of the reserved oil from the onions; set aside the rest. Mix thoroughly; the dough will be sticky. Add the eggs and 1 more cup of the flour. Mix lightly. Cover the bowl with a clean towel and and let the dough rise in a draft-free place (on top of the refrigerator) for about 1 hour, until the volume doubles.

Preheat the oven to 425° F. Place the rack on the lowest position in the oven. Turn the dough out onto a lightly floured board and knead it until it is smooth and elastic, adding as much of the remaining 1 cup of flour as necessary to keep the dough from sticking to your hands. Pat the dough out with your hands or use a rolling pin to fit into a 14-inch pizza pan, working the dough along the edges to form a rim. Let the dough rest for about 15 minutes.

Spoon the onions evenly over the dough. Sprinkle with the cheese, anchovies, and olives. Drizzle the reserved oil and herb mixture over everything. Bake for about 20 minutes, until the crust is brown.

Let the pissaladière sit for 5 minutes before cutting it into wedges. Serve with a glass of chilled dry white wine.

Calzone

This pizza turnover, which literally means stuffed pantaloons, was for many years an exclusive Neapolitan specialty and resembled the pantaloons worn by the locals. It's not clear how the idea of stuffing pizza dough to look like men's pants evolved, but it leads to some interesting speculation.

In this filling, the ricotta cheese predominates. If you prefer the more traditional mozzarella calzone, just change the cheese proportions.

½ **Pizza Dough recipe (page 98)**

1 cup ricotta cheese, drained, if necessary

1 egg yolk, slightly beaten

2 tablespoons grated Parmesan cheese

½ cup shredded mozzarella cheese

2 ounces Italian prosciutto, minced (about ½ cup)

Prepare the pizza dough as directed. While the dough is rising, prepare the filling and preheat the oven to 425° F. Prepare a baking sheet by lightly greasing it and dusting with cornmeal.

Combine all the filling ingredients and mix well. When the dough has risen, punch it down, and turn it out onto a lightly floured surface. Roll it into a 12-inch oval. The shape is important because you want the filling to extend all the way to the edge of the dough. Place the dough on the baking sheet with the long side of the oval along the edge of the pan, leaving half of the dough hanging over the edge.

Pile the filling on the dough, leaving a ½-inch border. Be sure the filling comes up to the border. Brush the edge of the dough with water, fold the other half of the dough over to form a large turnover. Be sure the dough is tightly sealed. Make 3 slits in the top of the pastry to let the steam escape.

Bake at 425° F. for 15 minutes; then reduce the heat to 350° F. and bake for another 15 minutes. If the dough becomes too brown, cover it with foil. Let the calzone stand at room temperature for 5 minutes before serving.

Oriental Noodles

Noodles are a staple throughout the Orient and India. Though they started as peasant food, they have been elevated, if not to haute cuisine, certainly to mainstream dining. Noodles are eaten as appetizers, in soup, as a main dish or a side dish; they even make very satisfying desserts.

If you have ever wondered why noodles throughout the Orient have a similar long, thin shape, it is because they are thought to be responsible for insuring longevity. This is particularly true in China, where it is considered bad luck to cut your noodles; you are, in effect, cutting your life. Perhaps this is why the accepted way of eating noodles is to shovel them into the mouth with chopsticks and slurp them down without biting them. In this way you can enjoy your noodles without challenging your propensity for a long life.

In China, noodles are often served for breakfast in a light broth. They are mild and agreeable, except for the very hot and spicy bits of pickled fish and vegetables sprinkled on top. These tidbits are guaranteed to open your eyes, if not your sinuses. This combination is an acquired taste for a westerner's palate, but the Chinese—even small Chinese children—bolt it down like corn flakes.

In China, every street market has noodle vendors. As a self-appointed noodle inspector, I pored over many noodle vats on the streets of Chinese cities. They are eaten throughout the day and evening—hot, cold, in broth, stir-fried, crisp-fried. Rice stick noodles, dried rice noodles, egg noodles, wheat noodles, cellophane noodles do not even make a small inroad in the variety available.

In Japan, noodles are a true fast food; they must be eaten quickly before they cool or become limp. The perfect noodles are served barely tender (what the Italians call *al dente*) in a scalding broth. Noodles are meant to be eaten with gusto. The loud sucking sound that the Japanese make while eating noodles is traditional. The intake of breath cools the noodles enough so that they can be eaten without destroying the roof of the mouth. If one eats noodles quietly it is a sign that they are not really being enjoyed.

There are as many different kinds of noodles in Japan as there are pastas in Italy. Their popularity varies by re-

gion. In the North, soba, the brownish-gray buckwheat noodles, are the favorite. South of Osaka, udon, the round or flat white wheat noodles, are eaten most often. Somen, kishimen, and hiyamugi noodles are used for special dishes.

In any large city in Japan, the appearance of noodle vendors is as predictable as the sunset. In fact, that is when they appear. They position themselves as close as possible to bars, where working men stop for a drink on the way home. Downing a bowl of noodles is part of the evening routine. After a drink and a snack, they are ready to face the night.

In Thailand, too, noodles are eaten in huge quantities. The Thais, who seem to eat all day long, eat them in many combinations: with meats, fish, vegetables, and various seasonings. They are eaten at home, on the street, at theaters, at political rallies, at sporting events.

Each vendor peddles one kind of noodle and often has a daily route through business and residential neighborhoods. Thai vendors handle their own advertising, announcing their presence with a unique lyrical call. People can wait for the cry of their favorite vendor, or change their menu from fresh rice noodles to egg noodles just by changing their supplier.

If it is spicy noodles that you want, all you have to do is walk the streets of any city in India. There, vendors sell crispy noodles that are made half of garbanzo flour and half of chili powder. Indians eat them along with a fresh green chile pepper, taking a bite of one and a bite of the other. One knows that the hot end of the scale has been reached when the top of one's head breaks out in perspiration while eating the noodles.

Chinese Noodles & Vegetables

Yield: 6 servings

Served at room temperature, these noodles can be eaten by themselves as a main dish; they also make a delicious accompaniment to an Oriental kebab.

1 pound fresh Chinese egg
  noodles
3 carrots, scraped and
  shredded
2 tablespoons peeled and
  shredded fresh ginger root
½ cup rice vinegar
¼ cup light soy sauce
2 teaspoons sugar
2 teaspoons salt
4 teaspoons sesame oil
2 cups shredded iceberg
  lettuce
4 scallions, cut diagonally in
  ½-inch pieces

Cook the noodles according to package directions until just tender; do not overcook. Drain and rinse with very hot water.

Steam the shredded carrots for a few minutes until just tender.

Make a sauce by combining the ginger root with the vinegar, soy sauce, sugar, salt, and sesame oil.

Toss the noodles with the carrots, lettuce, scallions, and sauce. Let the dish sit at room temperature until you are ready to serve.

Szechuan Noodles

Szechuan noodles can mean just about anything. It is fresh egg noodles with a sauce, and your choice of topping. Many vendors omit the toppings altogether and just serve it with a sprinkling of sesame oil, soy sauce, and a bit of chili paste.

Sauce

2 tablespoons sesame oil
2 tablespoons soy sauce
2 tablespoons red wine
  vinegar
1 tablespoon rice wine
1 teaspoon sugar
½ teaspoon chili paste
3 tablespoons sesame paste
  (tahina)
1 tablespoon minced fresh
  ginger root
2 garlic cloves, minced

Noodles

¾ pound fresh Chinese egg
  noodles
2 tablespoons sesame oil
1 boneless and skinless
  chicken breast, cooked
  and slivered
1 cucumber, peeled, seeded,
  and cut into thin strips
1 cup bean sprouts
2 tablespoons toasted sesame
  seeds

Combine all the sauce ingredients in a food processor or blender and process for 1 minute until smooth. Set aside.

Cook the noodles according to package directions until just tender. They cook very quickly; do not overcook. Drain in a colander and rinse with very hot water. Toss with the sesame oil.

To serve, toss the noodles with the sauce and the chicken, cucumber, and bean sprouts. Top with the sesame seeds. Serve at room temperature with a cold Chinese beer.

Chinese Noodle Soup

Early on cold mornings, university students line up right outside their school gates, holding their own enamel bowls and chopsticks. Vendors serve them steaming soup and noodles from large vats that are kept warm over a bed of white hot charcoal.

6 dried Chinese mushrooms
1 pound fresh Chinese egg
   noodles
2 tablespoons peanut oil
2 quarts well-seasoned
   chicken broth
2 tablespoons light soy sauce
½ teaspoon sugar
1 boneless and skinless
   chicken breast, slivered
2 tablespoons peanut oil
1 cup diced bamboo shoots
½ cup diced scallions
Bits of Chinese hot pickled
   vegetables (optional)

Soak the mushrooms in hot water to cover for about 30 minutes. Drain and cut into thin slivers. Discard the soaking water.

Cook the noodles according to package directions; do not overcook. Drain in a colander and rinse with very hot water.

Toss with 2 tablespoons of oil to keep the noodles from sticking. Heat the chicken broth to boiling.

Combine the soy sauce and sugar. Mix well and combine with the chicken slivers. Heat 2 tablespoons of oil in a wok, until almost smoking. Stir-fry the chicken mixture for about 30 seconds. Add the bamboo shoots and the slivered mushrooms and stir-fry for another 15 seconds.

In a deep bowl, place several spoonfuls of cooked noodles. Top with a little of the chicken mixture and cover with boiling broth. Add bits of diced scallions and hot pickled vegetables.

The noodles are eaten with chopsticks. Then, the bowl is upended and the broth is slurped noisily. The trick is to get it all into your mouth without letting it run down your chin and onto your shoes. It takes practice.

Fresh Rice Noodles

This noodle dish is a specialty on the streets of Singapore. The noodles, the sweet soy sauce, and the chili paste are available in Oriental food shops. Do not use more chili paste than the recipe calls for, until you taste it; it can anesthetize your palate.

½ pound fresh rice noodles,
   ⅛ inch wide
1 tablespoon sweet soy sauce
2 teaspoons sesame oil
¼ teaspoon chili paste
2 slices fresh ginger root,
   squeezed in a garlic press
½ teaspoon ground cumin

Heat 2 inches of water to boiling in a large saucepan. Place the noodles on an oiled rack or in a basket steamer over the boiling water. Cover and steam for 8 to 10 minutes.

Mix the remaining ingredients in a bowl. When the noodles are just tender, drain them in a colander and rinse them with hot water. Use your fingers to separate the noodles.

Mix the noodles and sauce thoroughly and serve at room temperature.

Pad Thai

Pad Thai is a classic Thai dish, with about as many variations as there are turkey stuffings in the U.S. Shrimp, chicken, or a combination of meats can be combined with the noodles. In Bangkok, pork is the preferred meat; in the provinces, dried shrimp and tofu are often used.

1 pound rice-stick noodles, ⅛ inch wide
¾ pound shrimp, chicken breast, lean pork, or a combination
½ cup fish sauce (nam pla)
⅓ cup sugar
½ cup white vinegar
1 teaspoon paprika
2 tablespoons soy sauce
¼ cup vegetable oil
3 garlic cloves, minced
1 tablespoon oil
3 eggs, slightly beaten
½ pound bean sprouts
6 scallions, thinly sliced
4 dried red chilies or 4 red serrano chilies, seeded, finely chopped, and pounded in a mortar
½ teaspoon salt
½ cup coarsely chopped roasted peanuts
½ cup fresh lime juice
Lime wedges

Soak the noodles in hot water to cover for 15 minutes. Drain thoroughly in a colander.

Peel and devein the shrimp, leaving the tail intact. Slice the chicken or pork against the grain into strips ⅛ inch wide and 2 inches long.

In a small saucepan, combine the fish sauce, sugar, vinegar, paprika, and soy sauce. Stir until the sugar is dissolved. Set the mixture aside.

Heat ¼ cup oil in a wok until it is very hot. Add the garlic and stir-fry until it is golden. Add the shrimp and/or the meat and stir-fry until the shrimp turn pink and the meat is cooked. Add the noodles and toss lightly to coat them with the oil and to distribute the meat and the garlic.

Bring the fish sauce mixture to a boil and add it to the noodles. Over medium heat, stir-fry gently until all of the liquid has been absorbed, taking care not to break the noodles.

In a medium-size skillet, heat the remaining 1 tablespoon oil and add the eggs. Move the skillet around to spread the eggs. Fry until the eggs are set but not dry. Remove the eggs from the skillet and slice into thin strips. Add to the noodles, incorporating them gently. Add the bean sprouts and the scallions and cook just 2 more minutes, until the bean sprouts and scallions are crisp-tender. Here too, use a light hand.

Combine the chilies and salt in the mortar and finely crush. Add to the noodle mixture and stir in gently but thoroughly.

Place the mixture on a large warm platter. Sprinkle with the peanuts and spoon lime juice over the top. Decorate with lime wedges.

Thai Fried Noodles

This is a simple version of Pad Thai. The addition of the salty dried shrimp gives it a distinctive taste.

½ pound rice-stick noodles
2 cups fresh bean sprouts
1 tablespoon dried shrimp
   (found in Oriental food
   markets)
¼ cup vegetable oil
2 garlic cloves, minced
½ pound large raw shrimp,
   cleaned and deveined
2 teaspoons sugar
1 tablespoon fish sauce (nam
   pla)
1 tablespoon soy sauce
2 eggs, slightly beaten
3 tablespoons coarsely
   chopped peanuts
2 tablespoon chopped
   scallions
2 tablespoons chopped fresh
   cilantro (fresh coriander
   or Chinese parsley)
Several lemon slices
Bean sprouts

Soak the noodles in hot water to cover for 15 minutes. Drain thoroughly in a colander. Soak 2 cups bean sprouts in ice water to firm them up.

In a mortar, pound the dried shrimp as fine as possible.

In large skillet, heat the oil, add the garlic and sauté until golden. Add the large shrimp and cook for 2 minutes. Combine the sugar, fish sauce, and soy sauce and add to the pan. Stir until thoroughly mixed. Add the eggs, peanuts, and noodles and stir-fry for 3 minutes. Drain the bean sprouts thoroughly and add to the skillet. Fry for just 1 or 2 minutes to heat through the sprouts.

Serve hot, sprinkled with scallions, cilantro, pounded dry shrimp, and lemon slices, and serve with additional raw bean sprouts on the side.

Mee Krob

This classic noodle dish is a mainstay throughout Thailand. If you think the amount of sugar is an error, it is not. In fact, this is one of the less sweet versions of this dish. It is an appealing mix of sweetness (from the sugar) saltiness (from the fish sauce) and hotness (from the chiles).

1 pound rice-stick noodles
Vegetable oil for deep frying
2 tablespoons vegetable oil
4 eggs, slightly beaten
1 cup sugar
⅓ cup white vinegar
½ cup vegetable oil
¼ cup soy sauce
¼ cup (or less) fish sauce (nam pla)
2 teaspoons paprika
¾ pound raw medium shrimp, peeled and deveined
2 chicken breasts, boned, skinned, and slivered
6 fresh serrano chiles, stemmed and sliced into very thin strips
1 cup bean sprouts
1 cup scallions, white part only, sliced lengthwise into very thin strips
2 tablespoons chopped fresh cilantro (fresh coriander or Chinese parsley)
1 orange, very thinly sliced

In a deep fryer, wok, or heavy skillet, heat the oil for deep-frying to 450° F.

Cut the noodles at the folds. Sprinkle them lightly with a little water. Unless you have a very large wok or skillet, you will have to fry the noodles in 2 batches. Add the noodles to the oil and fry until they are puffed and light brown on the bottom, about 20 seconds. Drain in a colander lined with paper towels.

In a large skillet over medium heat, heat the 2 tablespoons oil and pour in the eggs, moving the pan quickly to spread them evenly. Cook until the top is set, about 1 minute. Turn and cook another 30 seconds. Shred with a knife.

Combine the sugar, vinegar, ½ cup oil, soy sauce, fish sauce, and paprika in a wok or saucepan. Over high heat, boil until the mixture becomes syrupy, stirring frequently, about 5 minutes. Add the shrimp and the chicken and cook until they are just done, 2 to 3 minutes. Add the noodles and the shredded egg and mix gently until well coated. Try not to break the noodles.

Transfer the noodles to a platter and sprinkle with the chiles, bean sprouts, scallions, cilantro, and orange slices. Serve at once.

Transparent Noodles

This Thai recipe uses very thin noodles made of mung beans and water. They are a little chewier than rice noodles.

½ pound transparent noodles (found in Oriental specialty shops)
¼ cup vegetable oil
2 large garlic cloves, minced
½ pound lean pork, cut across the grain and slivered
½ pound cabbage, coarsely shredded
2 large celery stalks, cut diagonally into ½-inch pieces
2 large carrots, sliced very thin on the diagonal
2 tablespoons sesame oil
3 tablespoons fish sauce (nam pla)
1 tablespoon sugar
1 tablespoon vegetable oil
2 eggs, slightly beaten
6 scallions, sliced diagonally into 2-inch pieces
½ teaspoon black pepper
Lime Sauce

Soak the noodles in hot water to cover for 20 minutes. Drain them thoroughly in a colander and cut them into 3-inch-long pieces.

In a wok, heat the vegetable oil and stir-fry the garlic until it is golden. Add the pork and stir-fry until it is no longer pink. Add the cabbage, celery, and carrots, and stir-fry until they are crisp-tender, about 3 minutes. Add the noodles, sesame oil, fish sauce, and sugar and stir-fry until everything is thoroughly mixed.

In a small skillet, heat the remaining 1 tablespoon oil. Pour in the eggs, moving the pan quickly to spread them evenly. Cook until the top is set, about 1 minute. Turn and cook for another 30 seconds. Remove them from the pan and shred them with a knife. Stir the eggs into the noodles. Add the scallions and pepper and mix gently to incorporate all the ingredients.

Transfer the noodles to a warm platter and serve with the Lime Sauce in a separate bowl.

Lime Sauce

4 serrano chiles with seeds, finely chopped
⅓ cup fresh lime juice
3 tablespoons fish sauce (nam pla)

Combine the chiles with the lime juice and the fish sauce. Serve at once. This sauce does not keep well and should be used within 4 hours.

Soba in Peanut Sauce

These light buckwheat noodles easily absorb the flavors of the sauce. Linguine can be substituted.

½ cup water
¾ cup Japanese soy sauce
2 tablespoons dark brown sugar
2 tablespoons grated fresh ginger root
2 teaspoon dried cilantro (coriander leaves or Chinese parsley), crushed
1 tablespoon grated lemon peel
3 tablespoons peanut oil
1 cup thinly sliced scallions
3 tiny dried hot peppers, seeded and chopped, or ¼ teaspoon hot pepper flakes
1 tablespoon minced garlic
¾ cup roasted unsalted peanuts
½ cup fresh lemon juice
1 pound soba
2 large skinless and boneless chicken breasts, cooked and slivered
¼ cup rice vinegar
1 teaspoon white sugar
½ teaspoon salt
6 cups torn fresh spinach leaves
1 to 2 small hot red peppers, finely diced (optional)
1 tablespoon finely chopped cilantro (fresh coriander, Chinese parsley)

Combine the water, soy sauce, brown sugar, ginger root, cilantro, and lemon peel in a saucepan and blend. Place over medium heat and bring to a boil. Remove and set aside.

Heat the oil over medium heat. Add the scallions, hot peppers, and garlic and sauté until they soften. Transfer to a food processor or blender along with the peanuts and the soy sauce mixture. Blend until very smooth. Return to medium heat and bring to a boil, stirring constantly. Reduce the heat and simmer for 2 minutes. Cool slightly and add the lemon juice.

Cook the noodles according to package directions until just tender. Drain well in a colander and transfer them to a large bowl. Toss lightly with half the peanut sauce. Add the other half of the sauce to the chicken and blend well. This may be prepared ahead and stored in the refrigerator, but bring to room temperature before serving.

At serving time, combine the vinegar, white sugar, and salt and toss with spinach. Arrange the spinach around the edge of a platter. Place the noodles in the center and top with the chicken. Sprinkle with the finely diced pepper and cilantro.

Japanese Noodle Salad

Yield: 6 to 8 servings

Udon is a thick wheat noodle popular in the south of Japan.

1 ounce dried shiitake
   mushrooms (about 10)
Warm water
1 pound udon (wheat
   noodles)
5 tablespoons sesame oil
½ cup Japanese soy sauce
3 tablespoons rice vinegar
½ teaspoon crushed dried
   red pepper flakes
¼ cup chopped scallions
2 to 3 tablespoons chopped
   cilantro (fresh coriander,
   Chinese parsley)

Soak the mushrooms in warm water to cover for 1 hour. Squeeze to remove excess water. Discard the stems and thinly slice the caps.

Cook the noodles according to package directions until just tender. Drain immediately and rinse with cold water.

Over low heat, combine the noodles in a saucepan with the mushrooms, oil, soy sauce, vinegar, and pepper flakes. Toss gently for a few minutes to heat through. Place on a large platter and sprinkle with the scallions and cilantro.

This salad can be served at once or prepared ahead and kept in the refrigerator for a few hours. Bring it back to room temperature before serving.

Indonesian Fried Noodles

Indonesian cuisine is a blend of Chinese, Indian, and Middle Eastern influences. This noodle dish is surprisingly mild. At its most fiery, Indonesian cuisine can make your upper lip perspire.

½ pound fine dried egg
  noodles
¼ cup peanut oil
1 medium-size onion, finely
  chopped
3 garlic cloves, minced
½ large chicken breast, cut
  into strips about ¼ inch
  wide
¼ pound lean pork loin, cut
  into strips about ¼ inch
  wide
2 thin carrots, cut into
  paper-thin rounds
2 large cabbage leaves,
  shredded
2 celery stalks, thinly sliced
  on the diagonal (reserve
  the green leaves)
¼ pound small shrimp,
  cooked
¼ pound fresh bean sprouts,
  washed and drained
½ teaspoon freshly ground
  black pepper
¼ cup soy sauce
1 teaspoon brown sugar
2 medium-size tomatoes,
  peeled and coarsely
  chopped
6 scallions, coarsely chopped

Cook the noodles according to the package directions until they are just tender. Drain in a colander and rinse with cold water. Set aside.

In a wok over medium heat, heat the oil. Add the onion and garlic and sauté until golden. Add the chicken and pork and stir-fry for 2 minutes. Add the carrots, cabbage, and celery and stir-fry for 4 more minutes.

Add the shrimp, noodles, and bean sprouts and stir-fry until they are heated through. Season with the pepper, soy sauce, and sugar. Stir in the tomatoes and scallions. Stir for another minute, then serve topped with the reserved celery leaves.

Bits and Pieces

S ome street foods do not fit easily into a category. They are neither sandwiches nor noodles; they are not speared on a skewer, nor are they stuffed into a pocket. Nevertheless, chicken wings, fish and chips, tempura, and deep-fried potato chips are all important street foods. For want of a more precise classification, these worthy additions to *Street Food* are called "Bits and Pieces."

Chewy pretzels, roasted chestnuts, corn on the cob can be found on streets all over the world. In a sense, these simple offerings are the essence of street food. That's the way it was thousands of years ago, when an indigenous food cooked on the spot was sustenance for the hungry. If the food was also delicious, that was a bonus.

Today, it is the blend of cultures, as much as anything, that gives a street market its unique flavor. As a new specialty makes its way into the market, everyone moves over a little to make room for the newcomer's cart.

What entices normally prudent people back to street markets again and again? Part of the lure is undoubtedly the fragrance. The combined aroma of chestnuts roasting, potatoes frying, and chicken wings sizzling arouses the senses, whether you are hungry or not. Add a little nostalgia, and you are now dealing with a formidable yearning that cannot be denied. The only hope of resistance lies in the knowledge that you can make these tantalizing dishes at home.

A Short History of Pretzels

Pretzels have been around at least 1500 years, having started in the early days of Christianity. The tale told is that in an ancient monastery, a young monk, skilled as a baker, was preparing unleavened bread for Lent. Serious about his vow of poverty, he wasted nothing; even the scraps of leftover dough were not thrown away. He rolled them into a long rope, then twisted the rope to resemble people in prayer. (Christians at that time prayed by crossing their arms over their hearts and placing each hand on the opposite shoulder.) The twisted scraps of dough were baked along with the regular bread. He called his chewy innovation *pretiola*, so named because he used it as a "little reward" for children who correctly learned their prayers.

Pretzels were passed down through the centuries in the original shape. It was decided in the sixth or seventh century that the 3 holes in the pretzel *really* represented the trinity—the Father, the Son, and the Holy Ghost.

When the *pretiola* made its way to Germany it became *brezel* and finally *pretzel*. In the fifteenth century, German bakers used to travel around the countryside with a small baking oven mounted on a wagon, baking fresh pretzels on the spot. (Incidentally, if you ever see a recipe for *bretzels* in a Pennsylvania Dutch cookbook, it is not a misspelling, just the old German way of spelling pretzel.)

Apparently unaware that the Hungarians tell an almost identical story about croissants, the Viennese tell a tale of how in 1529, the pretzel bakers saved the city. The city was under siege by the Turks, who planned to conquer it by tunneling to its center in the dead of the night. But, the Turks did not figure on the vigilance of the Viennese pretzel bakers, who worked through the night to provide fresh pretzels for the following day.

The bakers heard strange noises of digging and scraping underground. They alerted the city, and after fierce fighting, the assailants were repulsed. Vienna was saved! For bravery and courage in battle, the Emperor of Austria awarded the pretzel bakers an honorary coat of arms, the lion — symbol of courage — combined with the twisted pretzel.

In Germany, pretzels have long had their own folklore and superstitions. To wish on a pretzel was a common custom in early marriage ceremonies. Much as the wishbone of a turkey is used today, if you broke off the bigger piece of the pretzel, your wish would surely come true. Pretzels were hung on trees to encourage the tree to bear well. Children wore them around their necks to ward off evil spirits. When parents decided that the spirits had been exorcised, the children were allowed to eat the pretzels.

When large numbers of Germans emigrated to the U.S., they brought their beloved pretzels with them. Pretzel aficionados in Philadelphia (the undisputed heartland of pretzeldom in the United States) pride themselves that recipes brought by German bakers have been retained to this day in all their chewy, crunchy deliciousness. What's more, today's pretzel vendors offer a choice of toppings: coarse salt, sesame seeds, or poppy seeds, along with the traditional slather of yellow mustard, which goes back to the days when the pretzel vendors traveled around the countryside in a wagon.

Chewy Soft Pretzels

People have enjoyed pretzels for hundreds of years, long before modern media began extolling their virtues — chewy and delicious, low in cholesterol, low in calories.

2 cups milk
1 package (1 tablespoon)
  active dry yeast
½ cup warm water
  (110° F.)
½ cup sugar
¼ cup vegetable oil
6¾ cups all-purpose flour
¾ teaspoon baking powder
1½ teaspoons salt
2 quarts water
3 tablespoons salt
1 egg
1 tablespoon water
4 teaspoons coarse salt
Sesame seeds (optional)
Poppy seeds (optional)

In a saucepan, scald the milk by warming over low heat until small bubbles begin to form around the side of the pan. Remove from the heat and cool to lukewarm.

In a large bowl, sprinkle the yeast over the warm water. Stir to dissolve. Add the cooled milk, sugar, and oil. Beat in 3 cups of flour to make a smooth batter. Cover and let rise in a warm place until double in size, about 45 minutes. Stir it down.

Mix the baking powder and 1½ teaspoons salt with 3 more cups of the flour. Stir into the batter, 1 cup at a time, to form a stiff dough. Turn out onto a well-floured board. Knead for 5 to 10 minutes, until the dough is smooth and elastic, using only as much of the remaining ¾ cup flour as needed to prevent sticking. Lightly flour the board and roll out the dough to make a 10-inch by 16-inch rectangle. With a sharp knife, cut the dough into 20 strips, each 16 inches long and ½ inch wide. With the palms of your hands, roll each strip into a rope. Keep the strips 16 inches long; the dough should be rounded. Work on a flat surface.

To shape the pretzel, make a loop of the dough with the ends pointing up. Cross the ends of the dough at the top, leaving a 3-inch tail on each end. Make the twist at the top and bring the left tail over to the right side of the loop and the right tail over to the left side of the loop. Press the ends firmly against the sides of the loop. This gives the traditional 3-hole pretzel shape.

Keep the remaining strips covered with a damp towel while shaping the pretzels. Repeat with the other strips. Place the formed pretzels on a lightly floured board and let them rise, uncovered, for about 30 minutes.

Meanwhile, in a large saucepan, start heating 2 quarts of water to boiling. Add 3 tablespoons salt and stir to dissolve. Preheat the oven to 400° F.

Using a large slotted spatula, lower the pretzels, one at a time into the gently boiling water. Let them boil for about 2 seconds. Lift them out and tilt to drain off all the water. Place the pretzels 1 to 2 inches apart on a well-greased cookie sheet. Beat the egg with 1 tablespoon water and brush the pretzel tops lightly. Sprinkle with coarse salt and poppy seeds or sesame seeds, if desired. Bake for 18 to 20 minutes or until the crust is golden. Eat them warm or cool.

Pretzels are traditionally served with a thick coating of spicy yellow mustard. These freeze well and can be reheated in a 250° F. oven.

Roasted Chestnuts

2 pounds chestnuts

Soak the chestnuts in cold water in the refrigerator for 1 to 2 hours. This helps to loosen the bond between the chestnut and the husk.

To roast, make a cross-slit in the pointed end of each chestnut, and place them in a wire basket. Roast the chestnuts over an open fire, shaking them often to distribute the heat evenly. Telling when they are done is a matter of judgment (unless you try the sixteenth century method described on the next page). They can also be placed in a roasting pan in a 400° F. oven for about 20 minutes. Chestnuts should turn a deep brown. Do not forget to peel them right away, even if they have been soaked in water beforehand.

Chestnuts: An Autumn Rite

Chestnut trees bearing edible fruit were growing in China at the dawn of history. Seedlings were first brought to Europe from Asia Minor during the time of the Roman Empire; soon chestnut trees proliferated all over the continent.

The pleasure of roasting chestnuts over an open fire is legendary, but to this day no good method has been devised to get the chestnut shell to give up the nut. Chestnuts have to be peeled while they are still warm or the nut will adhere to the shell forever.

Open fire roasting has another problem. How can one tell when the chestnuts are done? Chestnut lore has it that in the sixteenth century some clever lad thought of slitting all the chestnuts at the base but one, before roasting them. When the unslit one popped explosively in the fire, he knew that all the others were ready to eat.

The sound of exploding chestnuts must have been common enough for Shakespeare to have referred to it in *The Taming of the Shrew*. In Act 1 Scene 2, Petruchio compares a woman's tongue to the sound of chestnuts exploding in a farmer's fire.

Indians in North America were eating chestnuts when Columbus arrived. These delicious, nutritious nuts flourished no matter what the growing conditions, from New England to the Gulf of Mexico. But in the early twentieth century, they were killed off by a blight brought in by the Chinese chestnut. Today, most chestnuts come from the slopes of Mt. Etna in Sicily. The best and the biggest chestnuts of all come from France, where they are called *marrons*.

From remote European villages to the streets of San Francisco, the method of roasting chestnuts on the street is almost identical. The raw chestnuts are still slit at the base so they will not explode while they are roasting. They are then placed in a flat pan and slowly roasted over smoldering charcoal. The pan is shaken every so often to insure that the chestnuts will roast evenly. Chestnut vendors seem to have a sixth sense that tells them just when they are done. The practice of slitting all but one of the chestnuts does not seem to have survived to the twentieth century.

In cities throughout the world, one of the autumn pleasures is the appearance of the chestnut vendor. In New York, everyone knows that when the carts of roasting chestnuts appear, it's *really* time to put away the summer clothes; Christmas is practically here. Paris in October means that you can expect to find vendors standing near the metro exits, offering chestnuts, plain or coated with a melted butter and sugar syrup, to the homeward bound commuters. No one but the most resolute Spartan can resist the aroma of the roasting chestnuts and the sweet syrup. Commuters, one after another, decide that they must have a paper cone of chestnuts to warm their fingers and help them make it home.

Corn: On the Cob and Popped

Corn on the cob is one of the simplest and most widely enjoyed street foods. In the U.S. it means summer; it would be hard to imagine August without this mainstay. In Hungary, freshly boiled corn is sold by the gypsies. As far away as the beaches of Alexandria, Egypt, vendors squat behind little charcoal braziers and offer freshly roasted ears of corn with salt and butter to people walking by the seaside. On the beaches of Naples, the vendors are almost always old women, as they are along the roads of the Ivory Coast. There, freshly grilled corn is a special treat for children on their way home from school: nourishment for a penny.

There is some question about how "fresh" fresh corn should be, and it is best not to argue with those of the water-must-be-boiling-while-the-corn-is-picked persuasion. Of course, freshly picked corn will taste the best, but more important is the variety and age of the corn. Young, tender corn — boiled, steamed, or roasted — is so delicious that it brings tears to the eyes; older, tough kernels are not worth eating, no matter how fresh. It goes without saying that no corn is improved by aging it in a tub of hot water for hours, as some vendors do.

Just a few words about popcorn: America has had an ongoing love affair with this tasty snack food for a long time, at least since movie theater owners discovered that they could often make more money selling popcorn in the lobby than showing the movie in the theater. There is nothing one can say against popcorn; it is even nutritious.

Popcorn is one of the oldest snacks in the world. Remains of corn very similar to modern popcorn found in bat caves in central New Mexico date back about 5600 years. The American Indians were the first corn poppers in North America. They would toss kernels into a fire or hot ashes, and let the corn pop its way out. Another method was to place a whole ear of corn on a stick and hold it over the open fire until the kernels popped or burned, whichever came first. One wonders what their reaction would be if they were confronted with our designer popcorn, now available in exotic flavors. Chili popcorn? Nacho popcorn? Perhaps it is time for the popcorn lovers of the world to unite under the banner: "Stop Molesting Popcorn! Leave our perfect food alone!"

Grilled Corn on the Cob

Corn on the cob is elevated to haute cuisine when it is grilled. It is an order of magnitude better than boiled or steamed corn and well worth the bit of effort it takes to prepare it.

4 ears fresh sweet corn
¼ cup butter, softened
Salt and pepper to taste

Soak unhusked corn in water for 30 minutes. Peel back the husks and remove the corn silk. Combine the butter and seasonings and rub the mixture all over the corn. Fold the husks back over the corn and tie the tops with a strip of one of the outside leaves. Grill over a charcoal fire for 15 to 20 minutes, turning often until the corn is tender and the husks are almost charred. Remove the husks. It helps to have napkins, unless you enjoy licking buttery fingers.

Note: Although you lose the flavor the charcoal imparts, corn on the cob prepared in the microwave oven is absolutely delicious. To prepare the corn, use the instructions above and then follow the timing instructions for your microwave.

Deep-Fried Sweet Potato Chips Yield: 4 servings

Sweet potatoes and yams are eaten as a street food throughout the Caribbean and the Philippine Islands. Their preparation is almost identical in both places. In this recipe, a frying basket, which is part of a deep-fat fryer, is required.

2 pounds sweet potatoes or yams, preferably the cylindrically shaped ones
Vegetable oil for deep frying (about 1 quart)
Confectioners sugar or salt

Peel and cut the potatoes into paper-thin slices. Soak them in ice water for 15 minutes. Drain and dry thoroughly (important). Divide the potatoes into 3 batches.

Meanwhile, heat the oil in a deep-fryer until it reaches 375° F. Fry the potatoes in the frying basket, one batch at a time, until they are tender and brown along the edges, 4 to 5 minutes. Transfer the potatoes to paper towels to remove excess oil. Let the oil in the deep-fryer return to 375° F. before adding the next batch.

Serve the potatoes wrapped in a paper cone and sprinkle them lightly with confectioners sugar as they do in the Philippines or with salt, western style. Serve at once.

Belgian French Fries

There seems to be a pommes frites *stand on every street corner in Belgium. But, that does not stop some Scottish food historians from claiming that the improvement of double frying French fries was first introduced to the world in Dundee, Scotland, in the early 1860s, albeit by a Belgian who had a stall in a Dundee market. These fried potatoes made their way back to Belgium where they became a national favorite. Double frying became an integral part of the recipe. On a Belgian street, they will be served in a paper cone and doused with mayonnaise, if you don't stop them in time.*

6 large old potatoes, peeled
   (new ones do not deep-fry
   properly)
Coarse salt to taste
Vegetable oil for deep frying

Cut the potatoes lengthwise into strips about 2 inches long and ¼ inch wide; they should not be any thicker than that. Soak the potatoes in salted ice water for about 30 minutes. Drain and dry thoroughly (important). Use a kitchen towel to be sure that no moisture remains. Divide the potatoes into equal size batches of about 1 cup each.

Heat the oil to 350° F. Fry the potatoes in the oil, no more than 1 cup at a time, until they are tender but not brown, about 2 to 3 minutes. The potatoes should be limp. Drain them on paper towels and cool them thoroughly, but do not place them in the refrigerator.

At serving time, heat the oil to 390° F., and fry the potatoes in small batches until they are brown and crisp. Drain on paper towels and sprinkle them with salt. They should never be covered or they will become limp. Serve at once.

Fish and Chips: Simple Sustenance British Style

It is probably impossible, without causing a civil war in Britain, to resolve the time and place of the marriage of deep-fried fish and chipped potatoes. We know that by 1844, shops in the poorer districts of London were selling fried potatoes. At the same time, in the industrial towns of Lancashire and Yorkshire, enterprising piemen were branching out and offering fried cod with a baked potato, in addition to savory pies.

London, Dundee, and many beach resorts throughout Britain, all claim to be the true spot where baked potatoes first became fried potatoes and formed a permanent alliance with deep-fried fish. According to the Fish Fryers' Federation, the keeper of fish history and lore, Malin's in London's East End, which opened in 1868, was the first true fish and chips (chippie) shop.

At first, fish and chips was not considered a fitting street food since only the lower classes would eat it on the street—with salt and malt vinegar. The batter that fell off the fish while it was frying was sold (or given) to the poorest.

In Victorian times, when women came to the cities to work in the factories, fish and chips became a mainstay of their diet. Fish and potatoes were the cheapest of foods; frying made them more nourishing since it added the fat needed to help keep the women from freezing in their heatless dwellings. The fish and potatoes were fried in boiling beef drippings and wrapped in newspaper, which kept them warm and moist.

As fish and chips became more popular, they became more refined. Today, not many people would use drippings of the Sunday beef joint for frying; peanut oil or safflower oil have replaced the highly saturated meat fat. Haddock or cod are the most commonly used fish; flounder is elegant. Newspapers have been replaced by unprinted stock. Although nowadays you can't catch up on the news while walking and eating, the newsprint that was used for a hundred years would not be on anyone's good nutrition diet.

East End Fish and Chips

Salt and malt vinegar are still offered to enhance the taste of fish and chips, just as they were in the 1800s.

Batter

1 cup all-purpose flour
1 egg yolk
2 tablespoons beer
½ teaspoon salt
3 tablespoons milk
3 tablespoons cold water
1 egg white

Fish and Potatoes

2 pounds firm fish (haddock,
   sole, flounder), cut into
   3-inch serving pieces
2 pounds old baking
   potatoes, sliced lengthwise
   into strips about ½ inch
   thick
Vegetable oil for deep frying
Salt
Malt vinegar

Place the flour in a large mixing bowl. Make a well in the center and add the egg yolk, beer, and salt. Stir until well mixed. Combine the milk and the water and gradually add it to the flour mixture. Mix until smooth. Let the mixture rest at room temperature for 30 minutes. Beat the egg white until it forms stiff peaks and fold it into the batter gently and thoroughly.

Preheat the oven to 250° F. Line a cookie sheet with paper towels. Preheat the oil to 375° F. Dry the potatoes thoroughly and fry them in 3 or 4 batches in the hot oil until they are crisp and light brown, about 5 minutes. Be sure the oil is at 375° F. before adding each batch of potatoes. Drain the potatoes and transfer them to the cookie sheet and place in the oven to keep them warm.

Wash the fish in cold water and dry thoroughly. Drop 2 or 3 pieces at a time into the batter. Coat thoroughly; let the excess batter drip off. Be sure the temperature of the oil has returned to 375° F. Plunge the batter-coated pieces into the hot fat. Fry for 4 to 5 minutes, turning with tongs to prevent sticking. Drain on paper towels and serve immediately with the potatoes. Coarse salt and malt vinegar are the traditional accompaniments.

If you are a stickler for authenticity, serve the fish and chips in a paper cone of unprinted newspaper.

Japanese Tempura

When the Portuguese were banished from Japan in the 1600s, they left behind their deep-fried foods. Converting those greasy fried foods into an ethereal tempura was a transformation that only the delicate hands of the Japanese could accomplish. Using centuries-old frying techniques, a Japanese chef can bring out the subtle flavors of each food. The exact combination of cottonseed oil, peanut oil, and sesame oil is guarded as zealously as a successful perfumer will guard the secret of his famous essence.

Allow ½ to ¾ pound (total) shrimp and vegetables per person.

Shrimp and Vegetables

2 pounds raw shrimp (about 40), peeled and deveined, washed and patted dry
½ cup all-purpose flour
18 fresh snow peas
1 small eggplant (about ½ pound)
12 large white mushrooms
2 large sweet potatoes, peeled
18 small asparagus stalks, green portion only
1½ cups peanut oil
1½ cups vegetable oil
Lemon wedges (optional)
Salt (optional)
Tempura dipping sauce (available in Oriental food markets)

Batter

2 eggs
2 cups ice water
1⅔ cups all-purpose flour
⅛ teaspoon baking soda
1 teaspoon salt

Dip the shrimp into the ½ cup flour and shake off any excess. Remove the stem end and string from the snow peas. Slice the eggplant in half lengthwise and then into ¼-inch-thick slices. Slice the mushrooms in half. Slice the sweet potatoes into ¼-inch rounds. Slice the asparagus into 2-inch lengths on the diagonal.

In a deep-fryer, preheat the oil to 375° F. The temperature of the oil is crucial in this recipe and must not get below 350° F.

To make the batter, combine the eggs and the water and beat until frothy. Beat in 1⅔ cups flour, the baking soda, and salt and mix just enough to combine. You should have about 3 cups of batter; it should be very cold and a bit lumpy. The bowl of batter may be set into another bowl filled with ice. Use the batter immediately; it should not be held for more than 10 minutes.

Preheat the oven to 250° F. for keeping the tempura warm.

Using chopsticks or tongs, dip the prepared food into the batter, one piece at a time. Let it drip for a moment to get rid of excess batter, then drop it into the pan of hot oil. Turn with tongs or chopsticks after 1 minute and fry another minute until light gold; do not overcook. Fry just a few pieces at a time so the temperature of the oil will not drop. Remove the pieces from the oil as soon as they are cooked. Place the cooked food on crumbled paper towels on large cookie sheets. Hold the cooked pieces in the warm oven.

To serve, place a combination of all foods on each plate and serve immediately with lemon wedges and salt.

Note: The Japanese usually eat tempura with a special sauce made with a fish and seaweed broth (dashi). The dipping sauce is served in a small bowl alongside the tempura.

Tempura, Korean Style

In this vegetable tempura, all the ingredients are cut very small, combined with the batter, and deep-fried. It is eaten as a pancake.

2 medium-size potatoes, peeled and finely diced
4 scallions or one large onion, diced
1 green pepper, membranes removed, seeded and slivered
1 large carrot, julienned
1 large celery stalk, julienned
1 tablespoon vegetable oil
2 garlic cloves, crushed
2 small green chilies, finely diced
1¾ cups all-purpose flour
Salt and pepper
1½ cups water
2 cups vegetable oil

Prepare the potatoes, scallions, green pepper, carrot, and celery as directed. There should be about 4 cups of mixed dry vegetables. You can substitute other vegetables for the ones listed; be sure to cut them into very small pieces.

Heat 1 tablespoon of oil in a small skillet. Add the garlic and chilies and sauté for about 2 minutes; do not let them brown. Remove the pan from heat and drain.

In a large bowl, combine the flour and salt and pepper to taste. Stir in enough water to make a thick batter, stirring as little as possible. Add the sautéed garlic and chilies. Then add the vegetables. Adjust the seasonings; the mixture should be very spicy. Add more chilies, if desired.

In a large, heavy skillet, heat 2 inches of oil. When the oil is very hot but not smoking, drop in tablespoonfuls of batter. If the mixture is too thick and does not drop easily, add a little more water. Flatten to make 4-inch rounds, frying 3 or 4 at a time. Brown on all sides. The pancakes should not be thick or the potatoes will not be tender in the middle. Fry for 4 to 5 minutes, or until the potatoes are tender. Drain on paper towels. Serve immediately.

Buffalo Chicken Wings

Yield: 35 to 40 pieces

These famous chicken wings were hatched in the Anchor Bar in Buffalo, New York, and are now ubiquitous in bars and restaurants throughout that city. Though they may appear on the street in other cities, in Buffalo they are always eaten indoors. You are always offered a choice—mild, medium, or hot; the amount of the sauce is varied accordingly. The chicken wings can be deep-fried or baked. Deep-frying is more authentic and adds crispness, but baking cuts the calories. They make wonderful appetizers. In Buffalo, chicken wings are always served with celery and carrot sticks and a chunky blue cheese dip as a foil for the fiery wings.

3 pounds chicken wings
2 cups peanut oil or vegetable oil for deep frying
½ cup melted butter
¼ cup (or more) cayenne pepper sauce (Louisiana Red Hot Sauce, available in supermarkets)
1 cup Blue Cheese Dip
Celery and carrot sticks

Cut the chicken wings at the joints. Discard the smallest part (the tip). Wash the two larger pieces and pat them dry.

In a heavy deep-fryer, heat the oil to 375° F. Fry the wings, a few at a time, for about 5 minutes, until they are cooked through and crisp. Transfer the wings to paper towels to drain any excess oil. Be sure that the oil returns to 375° F. before adding more wings. Keep the cooked wings warm in a 250° F. oven.

Or, place the wings on a rack over a roasting pan, brush them with a little melted butter, and bake them at 425° F. until they are brown, 15 to 20 minutes, turning them after 10 minutes or so.

Combine the melted butter and the pepper sauce and toss with the chicken wings until they are well coated. The more sauce you use, the more fiery the wings. Serve hot with a bowl of Blue Cheese Dip and celery and carrot sticks on the side.

Blue Cheese Dip

¼ pound blue cheese
½ cup sour cream (or a combination of yogurt and sour cream)
¼ cup mayonnaise
Milk to thin

With a fork, coarsely crumble the blue cheese (you want the dip to have chunks of cheese). Combine with the sour cream and mayonnaise and enough milk to make a thick dip.

Jamaican Chicken Wings

Yield: 35 to 40 pieces

These wings are a perfect finger food and make a fine addition to a buffet supper.

5 pounds chicken wings, drumlets only (the largest, meatiest portion)
⅓ cup dark rum
3 tablespoons peanut oil
⅓ cup dark soy sauce
1 egg white, slightly beaten
2 tablespoons freshly grated fresh ginger root (not necessary to peel)
2 garlic cloves, finely minced
Flour for coating
2 cups peanut oil

Wash the chicken wings and pat them dry. Combine the rum, 3 tablespoons peanut oil, soy sauce, egg white, ginger, and garlic. Add the chicken wings and marinate in the refrigerator for 5 to 8 hours, or overnight, if possible. Remove the chicken from the marinade and pat dry with paper towels.

Lightly coat the chicken with the flour. Heat the oil to 375° F. in a deep fryer. Fry the wings, a few at a time, until they are crisp and golden, about 5 minutes. Be sure the oil has returned to 375° F. before adding the next batch of wings. Transfer the wings to paper towels to drain off any excess oil. Serve hot or at room temperature.

Note: Another way to prepare the wings is to marinate and coat them with flour as above. Then place them on a cookie sheet and bake in a 350° F. oven for 20 minutes. Frying them is tastier and makes a more authentic street food, but baking is easier and less caloric.

Tangy Chinese Wings

¾ cup dark soy sauce
1 tablespoon (or more) grated fresh ginger root
2 garlic cloves, finely minced
⅓ cup brown sugar
1 tablespoon Chinese mustard
5 pounds chicken wing drumlets (the largest, meatiest portion)
Garlic powder

Combine the soy sauce, ginger, garlic, brown sugar, and mustard. Mix well. Add the chicken wings and marinate them at room temperature for about 2 hours. Remove them from the marinade and pat dry. Sprinkle lightly with garlic powder. Place the wings on a cookie sheet and bake at 350° F. for 20 minutes. Serve hot or at room temperature as finger food.

Note: Chinese mustard can be purchased in an Oriental food store or easily prepared by combining equal parts powdered mustard (such as Coleman's) and warm water. Do not use regular, prepared mustard.

Sweets

Wherever street food is found, there are always vendors who zero in on our sweet tooth. The simplest sweets are fruits, found in markets throughout the world. Thanks to air freight, the exotic fruits first tasted in Mexico or in the Orient are now available in many large supermarkets. Just by inhaling the heady fragrance of a ripe papaya on the streets of Boston or San Francisco, one can relive that vacation in the Caribbean where an endless variety of exotic fruit was temptingly displayed by street vendors on every corner.

If simple fruits do not capture you, there are ice creams, ice pops, jelly apples, and crullers to tempt and tantalize. With just a little bit of curiosity, one can graduate to Belgian gaufres and Italian zeppoles. With all of these enticements, there cannot be many people left on earth who have not succumbed to a street sweet.

Jelly Apples

Candy apples, taffy apples, toffee apples are just other ways of saying jelly apples. And don't forget the caramel apples. These treats appear on the streets in the autumn, when the apples are at their snappiest.

8 to 10 crisp apples
Popsicle sticks or sturdy
  skewers
2 cups sugar
1 cup water
⅔ cup light corn syrup
¼ teaspoon cream of tartar
½ teaspoon lemon juice
Red food coloring

Wash and thoroughly dry the apples. Push the sticks halfway up each apple, through the bottom end.

In a 2-quart saucepan, combine the sugar, water, corn syrup, and cream of tartar. Cook over low heat, stirring constantly, until the sugar is dissolved. Cook the mixture, *without stirring*, until it turns pale yellow and is almost caramelized, about 310° F. on a candy thermometer. Remove the syrup from the heat and add the lemon juice. Place the saucepan in cold water for a minute, just to stop the boiling, then set the pan in hot water to keep the syrup from hardening. Add a few drops of food coloring.

Dip the apples into the syrup to coat completely. Put them on a greased surface, apple down, or stick them in a metal flower holder, apple up, until the syrup has solidified.

These are best eaten within an hour or two after preparation but can be kept covered with plastic wrap for a day.

Ice Cream: The Best of Our Frozen Assets

Ice cream is, hands down, the most popular street food in the world. There is nothing else that even comes close.

The history of ice cream goes back at least as far as the Roman Empire, when swift runners ran down the mountains to bring fresh snow to the emperor to be flavored with fruit juices . . . the first sorbet. Later, a frozen dessert, brought back to Italy from China by Marco Polo, became incorporated into the Italian cuisine.

When Italians emigrated to Britain they brought their version of ice cream with them. It was a grainy textured ice, halfway between a sherbet and a solid water ice—a sort of elegant slush—which was later given the more refined name of *granita*. In the late nineteenth century, Italian vendors fashioned small hand carts and pushed their tasty refreshment along English beaches; the carts advertised "Hokey-Pokey" in big letters.

Why hokey-pokey? Certainly these words were not part of the Italian lexicon. It turns out that hokey-pokey is the English corruption of "*O che poco*" (how little). The Italian vendors thought that they were passing along the information that their delicious ice, sold by the pennyworth, was also cheap. They never dreamed that hokey-pokey would creep into the English language without anyone knowing what was really meant.

The cry "hokey-pokey, penny a lump" became familiar, especially along the English beaches. Small white paper cups were filled with thin layers of sweetened shaved ice, built one on top of the other. No spoons were needed. Any child could figure out that the best way to consume this refreshment was to use the fingers to compress the paper cup, which of course, pushed the icy slush into the mouth.

Ice cream emigrated to the United States in the 1700s. It was in Philadelphia where George Washington first tasted it. The multi-talented Jefferson was one of the first to make his own ice cream, a skill he learned from a French chef.

The ice cream cone made its dripping debut at the St. Louis World's Fair in 1904, long before the paper napkin was invented. A Syrian immigrant, Ernest Hamwi, was selling *zalabia*, a waffle from his native country, at a booth right next to an ice cream stand. He watched the endless queue in front of his neighbor's kiosk. Everyone wanted ice cream; no one even noticed his waffles. When the ice cream vendor ran out of dishes, Hamwi, in the spirit of neighborliness, rolled one of his waffles into a cone and offered it as an ad hoc dish. This chance meeting resulted in a perfect marriage that will undoubtedly last forever.

The world's love affair with ice cream continues with unabated passion as new flavors and variations appear almost daily. Vanilla, chocolate, and strawberry ice cream (the originals) are now only three of a hundred different flavors. Luxurious designer ice creams that ignore calories and cholesterol are now available in every supermarket. These share the freezer with frozen yogurts that promise luscious taste, good nutrition, and, because of fewer calories, a svelte figure.

Italian Banana Gelato

Yield: 1 quart

Italians do something unique and wonderful to their ice cream. Though it is not as rich as the typical American ice cream, its flavor is more intense.
An ice cream maker is required for this recipe.

3 cups whole milk
¾ cup sugar
3 strips lemon peel, each
    about 2 inches long
    (yellow part only)
3-inch strip vanilla bean, or
    1 teaspoon vanilla extract
6 egg yolks
3 very ripe medium-size
    bananas
3 tablespoons lemon juice

In a 3-quart saucepan, combine the milk, sugar, lemon peel, and vanilla bean (do not add vanilla extract at this point). Stir over medium heat until the sugar is dissolved.

Place the egg yolks in medium-size bowl and beat them until blended, gradually adding 1 cup of the warm milk mixture. Pour the egg yolk mixture into the pan, combining it with the other 2 cups of milk, beating constantly. Continue to cook, stirring, until the custard coats the back of a metal spoon, about 10 minutes. Do not let it scald or the mixture will curdle.

Pour the custard through a fine mesh strainer into a large bowl. Discard the lemon peel and vanilla bean. (If you are using vanilla extract, add it now.) Cool to room temperature.

Puree the bananas and combine with the lemon juice. Place the mixture in a large bowl. Stir in 1 cup of the custard and continue stirring until well blended. Gradually stir in the rest of the custard mixture. Pour into an ice cream freezer and freeze according to the manufacturer's directions.

Gelato is best when served soft. If it stays in the freezer after it is finished, let it soften in the refrigerator for 15 minutes before scooping it.

Other fruit combinations can be substituted if preferred.

Italian Orange Ice

Yield: 1 pint

This comes pretty close to the taste of true Italian ice, vendor-style.

2 large sweet oranges, peeled, seeded, and membranes removed
½ cup frozen orange juice concentrate, thawed
1 cup water
1 envelope unflavored gelatin
1 cup sugar (or less)
⅓ cup freshly squeezed lemon juice, strained

Puree the oranges in a food processor or blender. Combine with the concentrate in a mixing bowl and set aside.

Place the water in a saucepan and sprinkle the gelatin on top. Bring it to a boil and stir in the sugar; stir until it is dissolved. Pour this into the orange mixture and add the lemon juice. Stir to blend. Pour into a shallow glass dish and freeze solid.

Remove the ice from the freezer and thaw until it is soft enough to cut with a knife. Cut it into cubes. With the food processor running, steel blade in place, drop the cubes into the machine and process until smooth and creamy. This can also be done in a blender. Serve it immediately or store in an airtight container in the freezer. Soften in the refrigerator for 30 minutes before serving. To serve, scoop into small balls.

Orange Ice Pops

Anyone who grew up in New York many years ago can recall the snowball man who magically appeared outside the school doors just as the 3 o'clock bell rang. It wasn't true ice cream but who cared? For two cents we could have a snowball water ice, shaved to order by the vendor, and topped with a choice of syrup, which he shook from a bottle. The syrup came in gorgeously lurid colors — cherry, orange, lime, and a blue concoction that dyed your lips indigo for the rest of the day.

The arch rival of the snowball man was the Popsicle man, who also knew when school was out. Popsicles were popular during the depression in the 1930s because they had 2 sticks and could be broken in half to provide a delicious treat for two. All for 5 cents.

Popsicles began in California in 1925. Two hunters (who were in the confection business) were spending a freezing night in the mountains. When they awoke in the morning, they found that they had inadvertently left a glass of orange juice with a spoon in it. It had frozen solid overnight. When they knocked the frozen juice out of the glass they had the first ice pop. Delicious, they said.

½ teaspoon unflavored
  gelatin
¼ cup cold water
¾ cup water
⅓ cup sugar
Juice of 2 oranges
2 teaspoons fresh lime juice

Sprinkle the gelatin over the cold water, stir, and set aside to allow the gelatin to soften.

Combine the ¾ cup water and sugar in a saucepan. Bring to a boil over high heat, stirring. Reduce the heat and keep at a slow boil for 5 minutes, without stirring. Remove from the heat and add the softened gelatin, stirring until it melts.

Pour the orange juice and the lime juice into a 2-cup measuring cup. Add the sugar-water mixture. Stir and set aside in the refrigerator to cool for 30 minutes.

Pour into ice pop molds and freeze until firm. Insert wooden sticks in the broad end when the ice pop is almost frozen.

Frozen Vanilla Yogurt

Frozen yogurt is a recent entry in the frozen dessert derby and worthy of attention.

2 eggs
⅔ cup milk
¼ cup honey
¼ cup sugar
2 (8-ounce) containers plain
    yogurt
2 tablespoons (or less) vanilla
    extract
½ cup chopped pecans

In the top of a double boiler, beat the eggs with a wire whisk until they are frothy. Add the milk and beat until the milk and the eggs are well combined. Stir in the honey and the sugar and combine well. Set the double boiler over the lower portion filled with simmering water. Place over medium heat to keep the water simmering and cook the custard until thickened, stirring constantly.

Place the custard in the refrigerator to cool, about 30 minutes. Stir in the yogurt, vanilla, and the chopped nuts.

Scrape the mixture into a freezer container, cover it tightly, and freeze for 1 hour. Remove from the freezer, stir to break up the frozen pieces. Cover tightly and return to the freezer for another hour. After 1 more hour, repeat and return to the freezer for 2 more hours or until firm.

Allow the frozen yogurt to mellow in the refrigerator for 30 minutes or until soft enough to serve.

This dish can be infinitely varied by substituting flavored yogurts and adding seasonal fruits. If you use fruit yogurt, omit the vanilla and add 2 tablespoons lemon juice.

Skewered Fruit

This originated in the Caribbean. Feel free to substitute whatever fruits you have on hand. Skewered fruit can be enjoyed as a snack or dessert.

½ cup brown sugar
¼ cup pineapple juice
¼ cup fresh orange juice
¼ teaspoon ground cloves
¼ teaspoon cardamom
3 tablespoons dark rum (optional)
1 large banana, cut into 1-inch chunks
1 large orange, peeled and cut into 1-inch chunks
¼ medium-size pineapple, cut into 1-inch chunks
2 nectarines, peeled and cut into 1-inch chunks
2 peaches, peeled and cut into 1-inch chunks

Combine the sugar, pineapple juice, orange juice, spices, and rum to make the marinade. Add the fruit and stir to coat. Cover and chill overnight, stirring a few times.

Drain the fruit, reserving the marinade. Thread chunks of fruit onto six 12-inch skewers. Broil for 10 minutes or less, 4 inches from the heat, until the edges of the fruit begin to turn brown, basting with the reserved marinade. This is somewhat drippy. Don't forget the napkins.

Waffles: Why Belgian?

Waffles are probably neither Belgian nor Dutch in origin, as both countries claim. According to the Scots, the waffle was invented quite inadvertently in 1204 when Sir Giles Whimple sat upon a freshly made oatcake while dressed in a suit of chain mail. How the waffle evolved from that unfortunate beginning and who first brought it to the continent are culinary mysteries.

We know that in France, waffles go back to the fifteenth century, when street vendors set up stalls near church doors during important religious festivals. The first waffles (gaufres) were cooked with religious motifs or in amusing shapes to tempt the celebrants.

Although waffles have been a popular street food in many European countries for hundreds of years, it is the Belgian waffle that seems to have captured our gastronomic loyalty. In fact, "Belgian waffle" seems to have become the generic term for any thick waffle. You see them in the most unlikely places; Mexico, Denmark, Hong Kong, the Philippines all have them. Of course the toppings vary: whipped cream in northern countries, exotic fruit toppings in warmer climates, sugar everywhere.

Belgian Gaufres

The Belgian waffle is thick, crusty on the outside and soft on the inside. The Belgians claim that you cannot get perfect results unless you use a Belgian waffle iron which can make waffles twice as thick as the American waffle. But this recipe comes pretty close to the real thing.

1 ounce fresh compressed yeast or 1½ packages (1½ tablespoons) active dry yeast

2 cups warm water (110° F.)

4 cups sifted all-purpose flour

4 eggs, separated

½ cup sugar

2 cups milk

10 tablespoons (½ cup plus 2 tablespoons) melted butter

½ teaspoon salt

1 tablespoon salad oil

1 teaspoon vanilla extract

Whipped cream, fruit, preserves, ice cream, sugar (in any combination)

Dissolve the yeast in the water. Put the flour in a large bowl. Stir in the egg yolks, sugar, and dissolved yeast. Beat in the milk, butter, salt, oil, and vanilla. Beat until the mixture is smooth. Beat the egg whites until they form stiff peaks. Fold them into the batter. Let the batter stand for 1 hour, stirring 4 times.

Preheat the waffle iron to 375° F. Pour the batter onto the hot iron, about ½ cup at a time, and bake until brown and crusty. Serve with whipped cream, fruit, preserves, ice cream, sugar, or any combination of these toppings.

Crêpes de Bretagne

Yield: 1½ dozen crêpes

Parisians munch these crêpes during the long afternoon to keep them on their feet between their early lunch and their late dinner. The crêpe vendors can usually be found at street corners.

In France, these crêpes are made of dark buckwheat flour, but that is not the same as the buckwheat flour available in the U.S. Don't try to use it. Instead, use a buckwheat pancake mix, which tastes almost the same. A large round griddle is used for cooking; the larger the griddle, the more authentic the crêpe. A heavy griddle, 14 to 15 inches across, is ideal. You want a large, very thin pancake.

1 cup buckwheat pancake mix
1 tablespoon granulated sugar
½ teaspoon cinnamon
½ teaspoon nutmeg
2 eggs, slightly beaten
1¾ cups whole milk (do not use skimmed)
1 tablespoon butter
Melted butter
Confectioners sugar, jam, or Grand Marnier

Combine the pancake mix with the granulated sugar, cinnamon, and nutmeg. Combine the eggs and the milk. Start adding the egg and milk mixture to the pancake mix, stirring constantly until you have a smooth but runny batter. Chill for 2 hours.

Over high heat, melt 1 tablespoon butter on a large cast iron griddle until bubbly. Do not let the butter brown. Place 2 large tablespoonfuls of batter in the center of the griddle and spread it very quickly with the edge of a thin spatula. The long thin spatula used for spreading icing works very well. As soon as the batter is set (just a few seconds) turn it over with a large wide spatula and cook on the other side for a few more seconds. Remove from griddle. Using a pastry brush, spread immediately with melted butter. A sprinkling of confectioners sugar, a little jam, and/or a squirt of Grand Marnier go on top. The crêpe is then folded in half and then half again and then rolled into a cornucopia and placed in a square of paper.

This is traditionally eaten while walking. Sweet cider is a delicious accompaniment.

Note: If you are making many pancakes, stack them between pieces of waxed paper and cover them with a towel to keep them warm, or place them in a 200° F. oven.

Mexican Bunuelos

Mexican bunuelos are crullers made of a simple batter, deep-fried, and sprinkled with cinnamon and sugar or confectioners sugar. Bunuelos can be made in the shape of rosettes; a special iron mold (found in cook's specialty shops) is needed for this cruller.

Bunuelos are very similar to the Spanish churros, which is not surprising, considering how closely akin the Mexican culture is to the Spanish. The big difference is that in Spain a mold is not used; the batter is dropped directly into a vat of boiling oil.

Vegetable oil for deep frying
2 cups water
1 egg, slightly beaten
2½ cups all-purpose flour
1 teaspoon salt
½ cup granulated sugar and
   2 tablespoons cinnamon or
   ½ cup confectioners sugar

Preheat the oil in a heavy saucepan or deep-fat fryer to 375° F.

Combine the water, egg, flour, and salt in a mixing bowl, food processor, or blender and blend until very smooth.

Place the rosette iron in the hot oil. Remove it and quickly dip it into the batter. Be careful to allow the batter to reach only to the top of the iron (do not dip the iron deep into the batter or it will not release while frying). Immediately lower the iron into the hot oil until the cruller slips off the iron. Fry only a few at a time for 45 seconds to 2 minutes (depending on size), until lightly golden.

Drain on paper towels and sprinkle with sugar and cinnamon or confectioners sugar. Serve at once.

Bunuelos will keep for 2 days in a sealed plastic bag, or they can be frozen. To serve, remove them from the freezer, thaw at room temperature, and heat for 5 minutes in a 250° F. oven.

Italian Zeppoles

These doughnuts from southern Italy are offered to celebrate St. Joseph's Day. They should be fried in lard to give them an authentic flavor.

1 cup warm water (110° F.)
1 package (1 tablespoon) active dry yeast
2 eggs
⅔ cup granulated sugar
1 teaspoon cinnamon
1 teaspoon salt
6 tablespoons butter, at room temperature, cut into small pieces
4½ cups all-purpose flour
Lard for deep frying
Confectioners sugar

Measure ¼ cup of the water into a small bowl and sprinkle the yeast over it. Let it stand for 3 to 4 minutes. Measure the remaining ¾ cup water into a large bowl. Add the eggs, granulated sugar, cinnamon, salt, and butter. Mix well. Beat in 1 cup of the flour, a little at a time, beating well after each addition. Beat in the dissolved yeast and the remaining 3½ cups of flour. Mix thoroughly. Knead until smooth and elastic. Place the dough in a greased bowl, cover it with a towel, and let it rise in a warm place until double in bulk, 1 to 2 hours. Punch down and let it rise until it doubles again, about 1 hour. Punch it down again.

Roll out the dough on a floured board until it is about ¼ inch thick. With a doughnut cutter, cut into 3-inch rings. Place the rings on a greased cookie sheet, cover them with a towel again, and let them rise in a warm place for 30 minutes.

In a deep-fryer, heat the lard to 375° F. Fry a few doughnuts at a time, turning once, until golden brown on both sides. Drain on paper towels, sprinkle with confectioners sugar, and serve immediately.

These doughnuts can be frozen. To serve, remove them from the freezer, thaw at room temperature, and heat for 5 minutes in a 250° F. oven.

Peruvian Picarones

Yield: 10 to 12 doughnuts

This doughnut uses oil, rather than lard, for deep frying, which makes it more suitable for those watching their cholesterol. The corn syrup gives it a luscious taste.

1 cup water
2 tablespoons butter or margarine
1 cup all-purpose flour
4 eggs, separated
1 teaspoon baking powder
Corn oil for deep frying
1 cup light corn syrup
Brandy to taste

Bring the water and butter to a boil. Add the flour and mix rapidly. Reduce the heat to low and continue stirring for 5 minutes. Remove from the heat and set aside to cool. Mix in the egg yolks, one at a time. Beat the egg whites to form soft peaks and fold into the flour mixture. Set aside for 20 minutes. Add the baking powder and fold it in gently.

Preheat 2 inches of oil in a heavy pan to 375° F. Dip your hand in salted water and pull off a small piece of dough about the size of a golf ball. Poke your finger through the center to make a hole and drop the dough ball into the hot oil. Do not crowd. As each picarone browns, turn it over. Remove from the oil and drain on paper towels.

Heat the corn syrup and combine with the brandy. Dunk the doughnuts into the mixture. Let the excess drip off. Serve immediately.

Funnel Cakes

These popular deep-fried fritters come from the Pennsylvania Dutch. When they were first brought to this country, funnel cakes were served as lunch for the farm workers, at 9 o'clock in the morning. (If the farmers were ready for lunch at that hour, when was breakfast?)

2 cups vegetable oil for deep frying
1 egg
⅔ cup milk
2 tablespoons granulated sugar
1⅓ cups sifted all-purpose flour
¼ teaspoon salt
2 teaspoons baking powder
Confectioners sugar

In a deep-fat fryer, preheat the oil to 375° F.

Beat the egg slightly; add the milk to the egg and beat until combined.

Sift together the granulated sugar, flour, salt, and baking powder. Add the egg-milk combination and beat until smooth. Pour the batter into a funnel with a ¾-inch opening; hold your finger over the bottom opening. Through the opening of the funnel, drop the batter into the hot oil, swirling the batter into circles, from the center out. Make each cake about 6 inches in diameter. Fry the funnel cakes until golden brown, turning once. Drain on paper towels. Sprinkle with confectioners sugar and serve.

Monster Cookies

Who first thought of baking a cookie that you need two hands to lift? It is safe to say that there is probably enough chocolate and nuts in these cookies to satisfy the ultimate craving. Monster cookies are an American invention. They probably will never become popular in Britain, where cookies are called biscuits. Somehow, monster biscuits do not roll off the tongue as easily as monster cookies, although they taste as good.

These monsters will be crunchier if the oats are toasted before they are added. If you prefer them soft and chewy, omit this step.

3 cups uncooked rolled oats (not quick-cooking)
¾ cup butter or margarine, at room temperature
½ cup dark brown sugar, tightly packed
1 egg, slightly beaten
¼ cup water
1 teaspoon vanilla extract
½ cup whole wheat flour
½ cup all-purpose flour
1 teaspoon salt
½ teaspoon baking soda
1 cup coarsely chopped walnuts
10 ounces chocolate chips (maxi-size, if possible)

To toast the oats, set the oven at 300° F. Position the oven rack in the center of the oven. Spread the oats on a cookie sheet and place the pan on the rack. Toast the oats for about 15 minutes, stirring frequently. They should be pale gold in color. Let the oats cool to room temperature.

In a large bowl, cream together the butter and the sugar. Add the egg, water, and vanilla. Mix until combined. Combine the flours, salt, and baking soda. Add to the creamed mixture. Fold in the oats, nuts, and chocolate chips. Mix until thoroughly combined. This process can be most easily done in an electric mixer.

Preheat the oven to 350° F. For each cookie, fill a ⅓-cup measuring cup with the dough and level the top. Drop it onto a lightly greased cookie sheet. With wet hands, shape and flatten slightly. Do not place more than 6 cookies on a sheet, fewer if the cookie sheet is small.

Bake in the preheated oven for 12 to 15 minutes, rotating the cookie sheet to insure even baking. Let the cookies cool for a minute on the cookie sheet and then remove to a rack with a wide spatula to finish cooling. These cookies can be eaten warm, at room temperature, or for a special treat, freeze them and then eat them frozen as you would a candy bar.

Sweet Noodle Kugel

In Israel, noodle kugel is a favorite street food. Though this is a dessert-like pudding, it is so full of good things that it is often eaten in the afternoon to help Israelis keep up their strength between meals.

3 ounces cream cheese, at
   room temperature
1 pound small-curd cottage
   cheese
3 cups whole milk
3 eggs, slightly beaten
2 tablespoons lemon juice
⅔ cup sugar
1 teaspoon salt
½ teaspoon cinnamon
½ teaspoon nutmeg
1 teaspoon vanilla extract
1 cup sour cream
¾ cup golden raisins
   (muscat, if possible)
8 ounces medium (¼-inch)
   noodles, uncooked
½ teaspoon cinnamon mixed
   with 2 tablespoons sugar
   for topping
Sour cream for topping
   (optional)

Mash the cream cheese with a fork. Combine it with the cottage cheese, milk, eggs, lemon juice, ⅔ cup sugar, salt, spices, vanilla, and 1 cup sour cream. Mix well. Combine with the raisins and uncooked noodles. Be sure the raisins are distributed evenly. Place in a well-buttered 9-inch by 13-inch baking dish.

Bake, covered, in a 325° F. oven for 30 minutes. Sprinkle with the sugar and cinnamon and bake, uncovered, for an additional 30 minutes, or until firm and light brown in color. Serve warm or cold, with or without a dollop of sour cream.

Drinks

Many of the beverages we enjoy today—beer, wine, liqueurs—were first provided by monks in abbeys where wayfarers paused to refresh themselves. Since thirst can be even a more compelling need than hunger, footsore pilgrims, who first began wandering about the earth, often sought drink before food.

The many references to the fruit of the vine in the Bible leaves no doubt that wine goes back to Biblical times. Beer, too, dates way back; it was the national drink of ancient Egypt. It must have packed quite a punch because it was said that those who drank it were so pleased that they sang and danced through the night.

Sparkling water was introduced in the late 1700s in England, but it did not become an instant hit; in fact, it languished for many years. In 1807 it was first produced in the United States: New Haven, Connecticut, can claim to be the American birthplace of soda water, later called soda pop because of the popping sound it made when the bottles of effervescent water were opened. For a while it was known as "belch water," but that seemed to evoke the wrong image.

The first batch of cola syrup was made in a three-legged cast-iron pot in the backyard of its creator, a druggist in Atlanta. It was sold in a pharmacy in downtown Atlanta in 1886, but it got a sort of ho-hum reception. Dr. Pemberton, the inventor, was happy to unload his interest in the syrup to Asa Chandler (of Coca-Cola fame). One can only speculate on what Asa Chandler's wife had to say when her husband told her that he bought a cola syrup recipe for $1700.

Neither she nor anyone else could have predicted that that purchase would redefine the meaning of refreshment. There is almost no place on earth that one can go, be it in a city in the U.S., a country village in China, or a remote jungle in Bolivia, where the soft drink has not preceded. One does not even have to know how to read to recognize the world-famous Coca-Cola sign. Anywhere on earth it means the same thing: Refreshment is at hand.

Although it is clear that human beings were successful in slaking their thirst up until the twentieth century without chilled drinks, there is no doubt that ice is to carbonated beverages what color is to television. If soft drinks needed any further improvement to corner the world thirst market, ice and modern refrigeration have provided it.

Coffee: It Didn't Start in a Cup

Long before it became a brew, coffee was a drug. In about the sixth century A.D., some Abyssinian monks in Ethiopia found, quite by chance, that when they chewed the red berries of the wild coffee bush, they were able to stay awake through their prayers, while their non-chewing brethren dozed. This difference was not lost on the chief monk, and the alert ones were suitably rewarded. Even in those days, it paid to stay awake. The monks soon figured out that it was something in the berries that prevented drowsiness.

Some time around the eleventh century, it became common practice to dunk the coffee beans in a ewer of hot water so that the goodness could flow out of them. The hot water was presented in a cup, and coffee became a beverage. The practice of roasting coffee beans (which are actually the dried seeds of the coffee cherry plant) did not start until the thirteenth century. From that time to the present day, there has been a continuing effort to refine and improve this king of beverages. Those who think that the addition of spices to coffee is something new should know that the Turks were experimenting with cinnamon and cloves in the sixteenth century.

The drink grew in popularity throughout the Arab world. It was carried to Mecca by the dervishes who drank lots of it for strength to whirl and howl during their devotions. Once the pleasures and the benefits of this infusion became known in Mecca, Muslim pilgrims spread it throughout Islam; Persia, Egypt, Turkey, and North Africa became ready markets (and growers) for coffee.

Coffee lovers owe a great debt to Louis XIV of France. It was he who was responsible for the proliferation of coffee throughout the western world. He fancied himself a coffee connoisseur, and when the king of Ethiopia gave him a small coffee plant, he carefully propagated it. The seedlings were sent to French colonies around the world. Descendants of those seedlings found their way to Spanish, Dutch, Portuguese, and British tropi-

cal colonies. Billions of coffee plants around the world can trace their ancestry to that one royal forebearer.

The effects of coffee have always been compared to the effects of wine. The lore is that wine makes us want to fight, make love, dance, and sleep, whereas coffee encourages us to talk, think, read, write, and work. Wine drinkers gamble; coffee drinkers play chess. In seventeenth-century England, coffee houses that were located near universities were often called penny universities. For the price of a coffee, one could participate in the ongoing seminars with the local intellectuals, all of whom seemed to spend part of their days in the coffee houses.

Coffee stalls became very popular throughout Britain and the rest of Europe. From Amsterdam to Madrid, a penny or two bought warmth, fragrance, and a slight caffeine buzz. Coffee stands and street cafés grew throughout the Orient, from Jakarta to Bangkok to Tokyo. On the streets of Singapore you can even find coffee with curries in it. Coffee has been one of the most enduring of street foods, as each new generation rediscovers its pleasures.

Lemon Sticks

Yield: 4 servings

This is the simplest of thirst quenchers, found on the streets of Philadelphia. The combination of flavors makes for a delicious drink. There are several imperatives: The lemons must be juicy and icy cold, and the peppermint sticks must be hollow in the middle so the juice can be sucked through it.

4 large juicy lemons
4 peppermint sticks with
  hollow centers

Place the lemons in the freezer for 30 minutes, or until they are almost frozen. Using an ice pick or a metal skewer, make a hole in the top of a lemon, about ¾ of the way. Do not go through the bottom of the lemon. Insert a peppermint stick. Serve immediately. Squeeze the lemon with your hand and suck the juice through the peppermint stick. On a hot summer day, the warmth of your hands defrosts the lemon, which in turn releases its thirst-quenching juice.

Cranberry Kvass

Kvass is the most popular street beverage throughout the Soviet Union. It is an effervescent and mildly alcoholic drink and is served very cold. There are many recipes for kvass but the most common kind is made by fermenting Russian black bread. Although black bread kvass is very popular with the workers throughout the Soviet Union, it has never caught on with non-Russians. If one hasn't grown up with this "bread beer," it is not likely to become a favorite beverage.

Kvass is sold out of big yellow tanks on street corners all over the Soviet Union. A woman, usually of ample proportions, sits next to her tank while people queue up in front of her to wait their turn to quench their thirst for a few kopeks. There is just one glass, which the woman swishes in a tub of cold water between users; no one seems to mind sharing a communal glass with hundreds of other thirsty Russians.

Much more palatable than black bread kvass, and very refreshing, is kvass made with prunes or cranberries. According to Russian folklore, to make a good kvass you must make it "angry" so it will bubble and effervesce. If you put some sugar and a few raisins into the mixture, you are sure to get the proper feisty brew. Kvass is a thirst quencher; it is not a sweet drink.

1 pound cranberries
7 cups boiling water
1 cup sugar
½ teaspoon cream of tartar
1 package (1 tablespoon)
   active dry yeast
6 raisins

Coarsely chop the cranberries (this can be done in a food processor). Place them in a large bowl and cover with the boiling water. Cover and let it stand for 12 hours.

Strain into a colander. Press down on the fruit very gently; there should not be any cranberry pulp in the liquid. Reserve the liquid; discard the cranberries.

Dissolve the yeast in a little of the reserved liquid. Add this to the rest of the liquid along with the sugar, cream of tartar, and raisins. Stir well to mix, cover, and let the mixture ferment in a warm place for 8 hours.

Strain the liquid and pour into a large bottle. Cover with a tight-fitting lid and refrigerate until ready to drink. Serve icy cold.

Smoothie

A smoothie is a perfect foil for garlicky or fiery street food. It is a very refreshing combination of fresh fruit and can be varied in the summer to fit what is in the market. Strawberries, raspberries, and blueberries, alone or in combination, make a delicious drink. In the winter, frozen fruit can be substituted.

1½ cups pureed raspberries, strawberries, blackberries, blueberries, alone or in combination
2 very ripe bananas, cut in chunks
Crushed ice
1 quart fresh apple cider

If you are using all raspberries or blackberries, strain the puree to get rid of some of the seeds. Then measure out 1½ cups. Process the bananas in a food processor or blender until smooth and combine with the berries. You should have 2 cups of fruit; you can vary the proportions of fruits to suit your taste.

Place ½ cup of the berry-banana mixture in the bottom of each of four 10-ounce glasses. Add 2 tablespoons of crushed ice. Fill the glasses with apple cider. Stir to combine. This should make a smoothie with the consistency of a milkshake. Serve immediately.

Egg Cream

An egg cream used to be a specialty of the corner candy stores in New York City when every candy store not only sold penny candy, newspapers, cigarettes, and imported cigars, but also had a marble-topped soda fountain. There you could perch on a high stool and savor a cold egg cream or an ice cream extravaganza. The egg cream has recently returned as a street food. Mostly in New York, but spreading fast, people are rediscovering this delicious drink.

An egg cream is not cream with an egg in it as I found out when I innocently asked for one in Massachusetts. In fact, it contains neither egg nor cream. It is a combination of chocolate syrup, ice cold milk, and seltzer, preferably poured from a proper siphon bottle. The designer seltzer that one buys in a six-pack could never fool anyone who has tasted the real thing. Also, an egg cream will not work with a rich heavy chocolate syrup; it has to be light in both color and consistency. If you can find the chocolate syrup with the unlikely name of Fox's U-Bet (sold in New York City), you have the basis for an ideal egg cream. A light syrup that says on the label that it is made of cocoa rather than chocolate gives similar results. The true egg cream should be served with thin streams of wayward chocolate foam dripping down the sides of the glass.

---

3 tablespoons light chocolate
  (cocoa) syrup
3 tablespoons ice cold milk
Ice cold seltzer

Measure the chocolate syrup and milk into a 16-ounce glass. Add enough seltzer to half fill the glass. Stir with a long-handled spoon. Here is the tricky part. Pour more seltzer from at least a foot over the glass, while stirring vigorously. You want to produce a foam that spills over the top of the glass. You can smooth the top of the glass with the spoon. Don't forget the napkin.

Almost Orange Julius

Although you cannot get the exact proportions from the people who invented this famous drink, it is not too hard to figure it out.

½ cup orange juice
  concentrate
1½ cups ice cold whole milk
¼ cup sugar
½ teaspoon salt
½ teaspoon vanilla extract
1 raw egg white (optional, if
  you like it very foamy)
8 large ice cubes, slightly
  crushed

Place all the ingredients in a blender. Blend until very smooth. Serve at once.

Index

H

Hamburger Melt, 58
Hamburgers, New Orleans, 30
Heroes, 36
Heroes, Meatball, 37
Hoagies. *See* Heroes
Hot dogs
  about, 41
  Crusty Corn Dogs, 26
  Texas Chili Dogs, 42

I

Ice, Italian Orange, 140
Ice cream. *See also* Ice; Ice Pops; Yogurt
  about, 138
  Gelato, Italian Banana, 139
Ice Pops, Orange, 141
Indian
  bhelpuris, pakoras, samosas, about, 83
  Curried Meat Samosas, 86
  Potato Samosas, Spicy, 84
  Tikka Kobobs, 15
Indonesian
  Fried Noodles, 116
  Pork Satays, Marinated, 18
  Satay Ajam, 16
Israeli, Falafel, 46
Israeli, Noodle Kugel, Sweet, 152
Italian
  Banana Gelato, 139
  Calzone, 102
  Heroes, 36
  Meatball Heroes, 37
  Mixed Grill Kebabs, 23
  Orange Ice, 140
  pizza, about, 96
  Pizza Margherita, 98
  Sausage Heroes, 38
  Zeppoles, 148

J

Jamaican Chicken Wings, 134
Jamaican Curried Goat, 22
Japanese
  Chicken Yakitori, 14
  Noodle Salad, 115
  Soba (noodles) in Peanut Sauce, 114
  Tempura, 130
  Tuna Teriyaki, 14

Jelly Apples, 137
Jewish. *See also* Israeli
  Cheese-Filled Knishes, 91
  Potato Dough Knishes, 93
  Potato Knishes, 92

K

Katjang Saos, for Satay Ajam, 16
Kebabs, 7–23
  about, 7
  Caribbean, 21
  Chicken, South Pacific, 20
  Chicken Yakitori, 14
  Corn Dogs, Crusty, 26
  Goat, Jamaican Curried, 22
  Mixed Grill, 23
  Pork, Chinese, 13
  Pork, Philippine Barbecued, 20
  Pork Satays, Bangkok, 19
  Pork Satays, Marinated, 18
  Pork and Sausage, Grilled, 25
  Satay Ajam, 16
  Shashlik, 12
  Shrimp with Feta, 11
  Souvlakia, 9
  Souvlakia Keftaides, 10
  Tikka Kobobs, 15
  Tuna Teriyaki, Japanese, 14
Knishes
  Cheese-Filled, 91
  Potato, 92
  Potato Dough, 93
Korean-Style Tempura, 132
Kugel, Sweet Noodle, 152
Kvass, Cranberry, 157

L

Lamb
  Caucasian Shashlik, 12
  Curried Meat Samosas, 86
  -Filled Gyros, 39
  Middle Eastern Kofta, 33
  Souvlakia, 9
  Souvlakia Keftaides, 10
  Tikka Kobobs, 15
Lemon Sticks, 156
Lime Sauce, for Stir-Fried Noodles, 113
Lumpias. *See also* Spring Rolls
  Filipino Shrimp, 74

Gingered Chicken on a Stick

2 Tablespoons vegetable oil
2 Tablespoons ginger root, minced
1 Tablespoon garlic, minced
2 chicken breasts, bone & skin removed & cut into long strips
2 Tablespoons soy sauce
1 Tablespoon honey
Sesame seeds for garnish

Heat oil in skillet (med. heat). Add ginger, garlic and chicken. Stir-fry for 2 to 3 minutes. Add soy sauce and honey - cook until chicken is done. Pierce the chicken strips on a wooden skewer & sprinkle with sesame seeds.

About the Author

Rose Grant grew up in New York City, where her taste for good food was honed, and her love of street foods developed. Her palate was further refined in gustatory heaven — Paris in the 1950s, which was awakening from a culinary slumber caused by World War II. She has traveled in Europe, Asia, and the Middle East, and lived abroad for several years — broadening her Jepicurean background and sampling street food wherever she went.

While living in Britain, she wrote articles about cooking for the prestigious British series Carriers's Kitchen. She has spent several weeks in China visiting hotels and restaurants in large cities (Shanghai and Beijing) and in the provinces. She had the unique opportunity of watching elaborate banquets being prepared with just a wok and a cleaver.

An enthusiastic researcher with a degree in library science, Rose Grant has a personal collection of over three hundred cookbooks. She is the author of Nitty Gritty's Fast and Delicious (1981) and combines her writing with professional cookbook indexing.

Today she makes her home in Eugene, Oregon, and spends as much time as possible in Woods Hole, Massachusetts.